Financial Discipleship @ Work

By Peter J. Briscoe

Copyright Peter J. Briscoe
ISBN: 9789083228532
November 2022
All rights reserved
Published by Compass – finances God's way
Zielhorsterweg 71,
3881 ZX Amersfoort, The Netherlands

www.compass1.eu

Foreword

Europe's best and most famous expert on the topic of Business Finance from a Christian perspective is Peter Briscoe. With this book he has he's outdone himself, again.

This book is a comprehensive guide and teaching about Business Finances from a Christian perspective. I think it should be the new standard and a mandatory read for all those who would like to educate themselves in Business finance from a Biblical perspective. It provides a biblical framework and criteria for making financial decisions. It gives you all the knowledge and wisdom you need as a Christian entrepreneur, business leader or professional in business dealing with financial issues.

One of the greatest contribution next to its practical application is that all the teaching is deeply rooted in The Bible and filled with profound Biblical wisdom and truth.

I think it is a must read for all business leaders who have to make financial decisions.. I can highly recommend this book!

Wouter Droppers, president Europartners, a movement of Christian business and professional people.

Contents

Part 3. Finance Decisions - by the Book

Part Four: How Can I Make Financial Disciples at Work?

About the Author

Peter Briscoe is an Englishman, born in 1950, and studied Industrial Chemistry and Management at Loughborough University of Technology, England. He moved to The Netherlands in 1974 and was asked by his company, Brent Chemicals International, to set up a subsidiary in Holland from 1978 where he was Managing Director until 1986.

From 1987-1989, Peter was Executive Director of the Christian Businessmen's Committees (CBMC in The Netherlands.) Typical CBMC activities are prayer breakfasts in boardrooms, hotels and even parliaments; outreach events such as banquets in major hotels to present Jesus Christ to the business and professional people; leadership development 'colleges', seminars and courses designed to motivate business leaders to reach out to others.

In 1990, Peter set up "Synthesys" a consulting company specialising in the development and marketing of industrial chemical specialties.

When the Berlin Wall collapsed and opportunities to develop business in Eastern Europe opened up, Peter founded and developed Europartners, a movement dedicated to reaching European business and professional people for Christ and helping Christians in positions of leadership in business, politics, and other professions to "go and make disciples in all nations." By 2002 there were local national movements in 28 European countries, encompassing around 500 local groups and some 5000 active co-workers.

From 2002, Peter took an assignment as Managing Director of HE Space Operations with offices in Houston, Katwijk and Bremen, specialised in providing professional services for Human Spaceflight activities. Peter led a company of some 70 people, made up of medical doctors, biologists, engineers, physicists and business specialists. Two new programmes in which the company is involved are the Galileo GPS satellite systems and the Journey to Mars programme "Aurora".

Peter is a co-founder of IAASS, the International Association for the Advancement of Space Safety.

Peter retired once again from business in 2008 to develop the ministry of Crown Financial Ministries and Crown Companies in Europe.

He served as International vice-president for Crown Financial Ministries coordinating Crown's global operations until 2012. This is being continued to date, under the new brand Compass – finances God's Way. Compass aims to help people in church and business to understand and apply Biblical principles of finance and business.

Peter is co-founder of Encour, a Dutch organisation dedicated to teaching Biblical principles on money, business and work. He also founded a movement in The Netherlands dedicated to train volunteers to help people to get out of debt, find gainful employment and become economically self-reliant. He was also co-founder of the Dutch National Prayer Breakfast, held annually before the opening of Parliament.

At home in Leiden, Peter is a member of the Leiden Baptist Church.He is married to his Dutch wife Didie since 1972 and they have three grown up daughters and are blessed with six grandchildren. Introduction

Introduction

I have been in business for over 40 years. I have been CEO of a chemical specialties company, started my own business as a consultant in chemical product development, and served as CEO for a company specialising in human spaceflight services. I have been a co-founder of the International Association for the Advancement of Space Safety, the European Economic Forum, our local Dutch National Prayer Breakfast, and a social enterprise to help people who are over-indebted. I also founded a European association of Christian businesspeople, which expanded into over 30 nations, and a European wide movement on financial discipleship.

Throughout my career, I have found that the way we handle money is key to effective discipleship. I have also experienced the difficulties in handling money faithfully. Money is very mischievous, tempting us to follow the world's ways instead of God's ways. I hope this book will be of some help to the Christian in business who seeks to follow Jesus as a dedicated follower, and to pass on what she or he has learned to others at work.

Business disciplines such as accounting, bookkeeping, financial planning, budgeting, forecasting are based on figures, but they represent a collection of decisions which have a major influence on relationships between people within and around our business and on our relationship to God.

We will look at financial decisions through relational glasses which have two lenses. One lens is focused on God and the other on those around us.

In Part 1, we will look at why finances are a key factor in our discipleship at work, and how we are invited to work in a partnership with the Lord.

In Part 2, we will look at the theological foundations of financial tasks, and the process of the creation, fall and redemption of financial disciplines.

In Part 3, we will look at making financial decisions – God's way and discuss ways in which financial decisions influence relationships and what effect they have on the health of the company.

In Part 4, we will discuss how we can make disciples at work, passing on to others what we have learned from Jesus

This study book has been written in relatively short chapters, which give a lot to consider. Look at the content pages and see which topics are most interesting for your personal situation, and dive in there!

Neither money, profit nor revenue is the goal of a Christian business. The goal must be to honour God, to give him the place that is his due both in our own personal lives and in our relationships. His priorities are about restoring relationships and developing them, so that God and his people can enjoy the best of each other! Financial management is not merely a technical exercise, but more importantly, it is a spiritual discipline for the Christian. It has been said that there are no financial problems, only spiritual problems, that are revealed in monetary terms and that financial problems can never be solved with money!

The goal of this book is to get the Christian in business to think about his or her role in the management of money within the business and to look at it through relational and spiritual glasses. The book will not offer ready-made solutions, but hopefully will inspire the readers to discuss their dilemmas with fellow Christians at work, so that they can develop their own leadership style in a way that will honour God and best serve the people within and around the business.

This study book has been written in relatively short chapters, which give a lot to consider. Look at the content pages and see which topics are most interesting for your personal situation, and dive in there!

Part One: Why is Financial Discipleship in the Workplace So Important?

In part one we will look at reasons why financial discipleship in the workplace is key for those disciples, working in businesses or other organisations, who handle money. It is vital for someone who is already following Christ and wants to express his or her faith in the workplace.

Chapter 1: Finances - the Key to Discipleship

Your faithfulness in handling money, is a key to open the door to living as a dedicated disciple! Jesus was clear, "If you have not been trustworthy in handling worldly wealth, who will trust you with true riches?" (Luke 16:11)

What did Jesus mean by 'true riches?' I believe that true riches are a dynamic, vibrant relationship with God, and all this brings. It brings the provision of the Father, the intimacy with the Son and the empowering of the Holy Spirit. Jesus is saying that the measure in which we will be able to embrace 'true riches' will be determined by how trustworthy we are in handling money.

Money is a huge day-to-day issue in our businesses. Many spend a majority of their waking hours making money, spending money, worrying about money, fighting over money, or trying to protect their money.

We think about money every day - several times - and this often causes anxiety and stress. The questions I hear most are 'do I have enough?', 'how much is enough?', 'Will I ever have enough?', and 'how can I get out of debt?' Anxiety and uncertainty can lead to inter-personal problems, health issues and decrease in spiritual involvement.

Living and working with Jesus, day by day, a disciple learns the will and ways of God from the unfolding challenges and lessons of life. Obeying each word spoken, they experience within themselves the renewing force and uplifting power of these words. The ongoing life of the disciple is characterised by Jesus's words. "If you hold to my teaching, you are really my disciples. Then you will know the truth, and the truth will set you free." (John 8:31,32)

No amount of money will ever set us free. We often think that to have more money will solve all our problems. When we think this, we are giving money power and devotion which only belongs to God - we are, in fact, loving money, which lies at the root of all evil. (1 Timothy 6:12)

Knowing the truth about what God says about money and financial problems will set us free. This truth is to be found in His Word, the Bible.

Jesus talked so much about money to His disciples because He knew how pivotal this is to their growth. Sixteen of the thirty-eight parables used a practical situation concerning money and possessions. In the Gospels, an estimated one out of ten verses (288 in all) deal directly with the subject of money. He discussed the topic of money more often than He spoke of faith and prayer combined.

Taboo

There is a strong reluctance to talk about money. It seems to be a very private matter and therefore not a topic to be discussed, especially not in church. Yet the Bible gives very clear warnings about what could happen when the topic of managing money is not addressed from a biblical perspective.

Very few Bible schools and theology courses devote any time to teaching about the handling of money and possessions. People surely need a biblical framework and criteria for making financial decisions? A failure to integrate Biblical teaching into our financial life leads to experiencing a crucial part of our life, which is not being influenced by the Spirit of God.

Therefore, we need to preach, teach and model financial discipleship.

Financial discipleship means to:
1. honour God as the owner of everything, (Lordship)
2. be good stewards of His resources, (Stewardship)
3. share what we are entrusted with for His purposes. (Generosity) and
4. pass on what we have learned to others. (Multiplication)

It is a calling for the believer to use our God given resources (time, money, talents, material resources etc.) for His purposes in His way for His glory.

Money management is not merely a technical exercise but especially a spiritual discipline. Following Jesus in our financial life should be a major topic of learning for all believers

Why financial discipleship?

Let's look at seven strong, Biblical reasons why we need to work with a biblical perspective on our relationship to money and material things.

1. Money is a major competitor for our devotions and seeks to divert us away from God.
"No one can serve two masters. Either you will hate the one and love the other, or you will be devoted to the one and despise the other. You cannot serve both God and money." (Matthew 6:24).

2. Money problems choke the Word and make it unfruitful as evidenced in the parable of the Sower.
"Still others, like seed sown among thorns, hear the word; but the worries of this life, the deceitfulness of wealth and the desires for other things come in and choke the word, making it unfruitful" (Mark 4: 18-19).

3. The way we use our money is an outside indicator of an inside spiritual state.
"For where your treasure is, there your heart will be also". (Matthew 6:21).

4. The love of money lies at the root of all kinds of evil
"For the love of money is a root of all kinds of evil. Some people, eager for money, have wandered from the faith and pierced themselves with many griefs." (1 Timothy 6:10).

5. Inability to pay back debt robs you of your freedom.
"Just as the rich rule over the poor, so the borrower becomes slave to the lender." (Proverbs 22:7).

6. The measure by which God entrusts to us His true riches is determined by the way we handle money.
"Whoever can be trusted with very little can also be trusted with much, and whoever is dishonest with very little will also be dishonest with much. So if you have not been trustworthy in handling worldly wealth, who will trust you with true riches? And if you have not been trustworthy with someone else's property, who will give you property of your own?" (Luke 16:10-12).

7. Lack of knowledge negatively influences our life and work. "Your people are destroyed for lack of knowledge..." Hosea (4:6)

Priorities

The way we spend our money is a direct reflection of our heart's priorities. It cannot be faked - we can read this in black and white on our bank statements. The author G. K. Chesterton once said, "Show me the stubs in a man's check book and I will tell you what he cares about."[1]

Billy Graham put it a little differently, "Give me five minutes with a person's check book, and I will tell you where their heart is."[2] Most people don't have a check book anymore, but you get the idea.

Money is one way that our priorities and values are made visible.

Godfrey Davis, who wrote a biography about the Duke of Wellington, said, "I found an old account ledger that showed how the duke spent his money. It was a far better clue to what he thought was really important than reading his letters or speeches."[3]

How we choose to use money provides a window into the soul. As a resource, money allows us to amplify and what's inside of us and enables us to put this into practice.

Presumably what we invest in is what's most important in our lives. Jesus is concerned about our heart, the centre of our being, and the fruit which the Spirit causes to spring out of our hearts. Money is not fruit, but the way we use our money should be an expression of the fruit of the Spirit. That's why financial discipleship is so important.

It is said the finances are the 'funny bone' of discipleship. A funny bone is a part in the elbow over which a sensitive nerve passes. If the elbow is knocked on a hard table or door, you can experience a shock pain, tingling and numbness. The pain can radiate along the whole arm into the fingers. Actually, there's nothing funny about it!

Financial management in the workplace

Financial management is one of the most important responsibilities of managers or entrepreneurs. Those handling money must consider the consequences of their decisions on profits, cash flow and on the financial health of the company. All business activities have an impact on the company's financial state and the responsible managers must keep abreast of financial developments.

The Biblical word for 'manager' or a 'steward' is 'Oikonomos,' from which we get our word, economist. According to the Greek Lexicon, the definition of 'oikonomos' is; "A steward, manager, superintendent, to whom the head of the house or proprietor has entrusted the management of his affairs, the care of receipts and expenditures, and the duty of dealing out the proper portion to every servant; the manager of a farm or landed estate, an overseer; the superintendent of the city's finances, the treasurer of a city or treasurers of kings. 4
Any person in an organisation who has some responsibility for handling money is an 'oikonomos.'

Jesus told a parable about a master coming home from being away at a wedding. He praised those servants who are ready to receive the master and who have looked after the household while he was away. Jesus then gave a good job description of a financial disciple. "And the Lord said, "Who then is the faithful and wise manager, whom his master will set over his household, to give them their portion of food at the proper time? Blessed is that servant whom his master will find so doing when he comes. Truly, I say to you, he will set him over all his possessions." (Luke 12:42,43)

From this, we can conclude that the faithful and wise manager pays salaries and bills on time. There are many people who are dependent on an organisation for their livelihood. I know from years of personal experience how important it is to pay what is due, fully and on time. Also, how much anxiety and concern can be caused when this does not happen. More on this later.

Chapter 2: Problems in the Workplace

Financial discipleship is so important in the workplace because many problems occur due to mismanagement, corruption, fraud or dishonesty. Many co-workers have serious financial problems in their private lives. This can have serious effects on their mental and physical health, leading to loss of productivity and satisfaction in their work.

Financial mismanagement

Financial mismanagement often occurs when money is handled in a way that can be characterised as "wrong, bad, careless, inefficient or incompetent" and negatively affects the financial standing of a business or individual.

A lack of good financial management is a big reason why companies do not survive. This could be due to the wrong distribution of responsibility, not paying bills and taxes on time, not paying attention to maintaining a healthy cash flow, or reserving for necessary investments.

Here are some problems with financial mismanagement.
1. You cannot know if your business is even profitable.
   If you are not tracking what's coming in or going out, you have no idea if your sales or offers are even profitable.
2. Your costs could become too high.
   Costs running too high can kill an organisation. If you are aware of overspending, you can make adjustments.
3. You could run out of cash.
   Maintaining a positive cash flow is essential to enable you to meet all your obligations, fully and on time. When the flow of cash dries up, your business is in trouble, despite being profitable.
4. You cannot make well-informed decisions.
   In order to make wise decisions you need accurate, current information on the financial consequences of decisions made within the organisation.
5. Your ability to get investment is damaged.
   Accurate financial statements are essential to show investors or lenders that they can invest in your business.

Dishonesty

Dishonesty in the workplace shows itself in many ways, such as employee theft, submitting incorrect time sheets, cheating on expenses, stealing company property, and lying. Dishonesty in the workplace can result in lost revenue, decreased productivity and low morale.

Employees who are dissatisfied with their jobs, or the way the company is being led or by their working conditions could easily start stealing, lying or cheating.

Fraud usually occurs when employees are pressured financially or emotionally and have the opportunity to steal. Many employees start fraud by 'borrowing' money with the intent of giving it back, but if not caught, continue to take more and more. Those that commit fraud can easily rationalise stealing money, like rationalising telling white lies. Regardless of the situation, lying is a slippery slope, a banana skin that can cause us to slip up with severe consequences on both the employee and business.

Corruption

Corruption is when people in positions of power engage in unethical and illegal activities for personal gain and taking undue advantage of those in a weaker position.

Corruption has many faces and is not always obvious but takes on subtle forms. Some forms of corruption are quite common and unfortunately often accepted as a necessary evil in order to be able to conduct business.

Customers and consumers end up paying a higher price, and competitors suffer due to an unequal playing field.

Here are some examples of the many types of corruption:

- Bribery: accepting items in return for unfair priority treatment
- Fraud: wrongful or criminal deception intended to result in financial or personal gain.
- Embezzlement: the act of withholding or stealing assets for the purpose of selling those assets, by one or more persons to whom the assets were entrusted,
- Kickbacks: illegal payments intended as compensation for preferential treatment, or any other

type of improper services received.

It is important to distinguish between a bribe and a business gift.

- A gift is something given without expecting anything in return. A bribe is the same given in the hope to benefit from it.
- A gift is when something is given to reward good performance in the past. A bribe has the intended purpose of influencing someone to get a favourable business decision in the future.

Cost of corruption

The Global Corruption Barometer shows that more than one in four people worldwide reported having paid a bribe within the past year when interacting with public institutions. More than half of the people surveyed said their governments are ineffective at fighting the problem.[5]

A major 2021 study, published by the University of Portsmouth Centre for Counter Fraud Studies, revealed that fraud now costs UK businesses and individuals more than £137 billion a year.

Jim Gee, a forensic accountant said in the study; "These sums are stark but may be hard to grasp. In the UK alone, the amount lost to fraud outweighs the wealth of Jeff Bezos, while the amount lost to fraud globally represents more than twice the UK's entire GDP.

Too many organisations adopt a reactive approach to fraud, seeking only to tackle it once losses have already occurred. That's an antiquated viewpoint and a change of perspective is needed."[6]

The global accounting giant, PwC's Global Economic Crime and Fraud Survey 2020, showed evidence that 47% of companies experienced a fraud in the past 24 months. They reported an average of 6 frauds per company.

The total cost for 5,000 respondents across 99 territories worldwide over the past 24 months was an eye-watering US$42 billion. That's cash taken straight off companies' bottom line. And 13% of those who'd experienced a fraud said they'd lost US$50 million-plus. The threat of fraud is current and growing. [7]

Financial stress of employees

Delegates at a 2018 symposium by the insurance giant, MetLife, on 'Rethinking employee financial wellness,' were told that:

"The impact of personal financial problems on workplace wellness is a 'hidden epidemic,' with serious risks for employers from lost productivity and relationships with customers. [8]

A large survey done by the Netherlands Institute for financial well-being, in 2017 shows that 62 percent of employers have to deal with staff who have financial problems. An employer can easily spend €13,000 per year on an employee with financial problems who works full-time and earns an average salary. Employers only get a late insight into the financial problems of their staff.

57 percent of employers see staff with debts as a major risk for the organisation. The costs are mainly in the processing of wage advancements or garnishment or, (sickness) absence and loss of productivity. In addition, the company may be at risk from theft, fraud, and the fact that staff with money problems are more susceptible to bribery and blackmail.

The major outcomes of the report were:
- A third of the employers consider financial problems of employees as a reason not to extend a contract.
- Almost one in five sees it as a reason for dismissal.
- More than half of the employers think that employees are afraid of this.
- Three quarters of employers feel that the financial health of employees is an important part of HR policy.
- Eighty per cent of employers are happy to support employees with money problems. [9]

PwC's 2021 Employee Financial Wellness Survey showed that 63% of employees say that their financial stress has increased since the start of the recent pandemic.

Since nearly 60 percent of employees in the U.S. say they are financially stressed—more than all other life stressors combined—employers should not only be concerned about this problem, but also actively trying to solve it.

Studies show that financially stressed employees are less productive, more distracted, produce lower-quality work, have poorer relationships with co-workers and have higher rates of absenteeism and on-the-job accidents.

The survey revealed that employees are unprepared for an extended economic downturn or recession: Many employees are already in a fragile financial state and unprepared for short-term cash needs, lacking the ability to absorb even a minor shock. In fact, more than one-third of full-time employed Millennials, Gen Xers, and Baby Boomers, have less than $1,000 saved to deal with unexpected expenses. [10]

Financial stress has been linked to post-traumatic stress

disorder, substance abuse disorder, suicide, and mental health disorders, especially among millennials.

U.S. businesses are losing $500 billion a year because of employees' personal financial stress, according to a survey by salaryfinance.com.[11]
Financially stressed employees are two times less likely to get enough sleep, exercise regularly, get a flu shot, go to the doctor and dentist, eat healthy, maintain a healthy weight, and avoid tobacco use.
Employers can end up paying more due to higher use of employee assistance programs, higher health care costs, increased absenteeism, and more on-the-job, stress-related employee accidents.
Employees experiencing financial stress are more likely to habitually miss work. Absenteeism costs U.S. companies a whopping $226 billion a year, according to the CDC Foundation.

A Fidelity Investments 'well-being' survey of more than 9,300 people found that employees with the highest levels of debt were twice as likely to miss work as those with the lowest debt levels. [12]

'Presenteeism' is a term used for employees who are physically present at work but performing their jobs at less than full capacity. Presenteeism shows itself in a number of ways, including high levels of distraction, low engagement with work and colleagues, poor work quality and declining job performance.
The 2019 PWC Employee Financial Wellness Survey found that 35 percent of employees were distracted at work due to finances. Of those distracted, nearly half spent 3 or more hours per week handling financial issues.[13]

Financial problems are opportunities

Opportunities are wrapped up in problems. Identifying people at work with personal financial problems presents an opportunity to get alongside them and offer help. Help could come from a budget coach, invitation to a Compass course or a company sponsored workshop on 'financial fitness.'

Many communise are building employee financial fitness programs into their HR policies.

I remember our company wanting to help a young, single mother with financial problems which were affecting her work. Due to the wage structure in our business, we could not offer her a salary increase. We contacted her church and made a donation by which the church could help her through a tough period.

Financial problems often reveal an outward indication of internal problems." These problems could be of a psychological or a spiritual nature. Helping them can open a door to helping them get their lives sorted, become internally stronger and oftentimes grow spiritually.

Keeping our eyes open and looking out for people with financial problems can be our invitation to step into their lives and help them get to know God's ways of dealing with finances!

Chapter 3: Working in Partnership

God owns everything - His creation, of course, but also myself, my dreams, my skills and talents and my career. The resources I have in my possession belong to God. "You do not belong to yourself, for God bought you and everything you control, with a high price. Therefore, you must honour God with all you are, all you do, and with everything you have." (My version of 1 Corinthians 6:19)

Jesus was very clear about the cost of becoming His disciple. "If you want to be my disciple, you must, by comparison, hate everyone else—your father and mother, wife and children, brothers and sisters—yes, even your own life. Otherwise, you cannot be my disciple. And if you do not carry your own cross and follow me, you cannot be my disciple. So you cannot become my disciple without giving up everything you own." (Luke 14:26 & 33)

When we surrender and renounce possession of these things, the Lord says as it were, "Thank you, my son/daughter. Now let's get working together in a new partnership. You are no longer on your own. Let's get to work - together!

The Lord is the lead partner, and I am invited to work with him, learn from him and experience all the fruit which that will bring.

Do you remember the last time that you signed over the deed or title of something that you owned? The last time you sold a car, you signed over the car title. When you sold your last house, you signed over the deed at closing. Have you ever sold a business or a commercial property? With a property we may do that quite casually and be glad to get rid of the debt and make some cash.

One of my most important mentors, Kent Humphreys, told me of the time when, in 1997, he signed over ownership of the distribution firm which his family had owned for 38 years.

"It took me about 45 minutes to sign papers on two or three long tables. The next day I was still CEO, but someone else owned the firm. I then had a stewardship position, I still felt responsible and wanted to succeed, but a huge burden was lifted from my shoulders.

I was no longer ultimately responsible for the debt, the livelihood of four hundred families, and the final decision. I was accountable to the owner to run it properly.

I remember a meeting of twelve business owners in Kuala Lumpur, Malaysia, in which they signed over the deed to their businesses to Jesus Christ. It was a special privilege for me to be there. Four local pastors were also present. Each company owner read the deed and signed it. The pastors prayed for each business steward individually. Then we prayed, laid hands on the pastors, and commissioned them to be involved in the equipping of each CEO to run their business for Christ. Finally, the pastors prayed for the group of leaders as a whole that their actions would impact the companies, the city, and the nation. We had two witnesses sign each deed and took photos to help remind all involved.

They assumed the role of CEO as stewards, no longer owners. Every decision must now be made in the best interest of the owner, Jesus Christ. They must be obedient stewards and be honest and faithful CEO's. However, Christ is the owner, and He will make the final major decisions. That takes the pressure off. All we have to do is submit to His vision, mission, principles, and leadership."

If you feel led to do the same as these Malaysian leaders, just adapt the form below. Have witnesses sign the deed with you. Make sure that your peers hold you accountable.

You can also do this if you do not own a company yourself. In this case you have your career and your authority to surrender.

I remember attending a ceremony in Rotterdam when a good friend invited his spouse, pastor, and key employees to attend the ceremony of dedication of the company to the Lord.

Dedication of Business

I < your name> the legal owner/part-owner of < Company > solemnly declare before everyone present, and before all Heaven and Earth that I on this day willingly transfer the ownership of this company over to the Almighty God, the creator of all things.

I believe that God, my heavenly Father desires that all things be reconciled back to Him through His Son Jesus Christ. As of today, I acknowledge that God is the rightful owner of <Company> and I am now His steward looking after His resources.

Therefore, I now repent of all the past wrong doings done by < Company >; it's owners, officers and employees and ask you God to forgive us and cleanse us by the blood of your son Jesus Christ. God, I ask you to redeem < Company >, all its assets and reputation so that it can be used to bring glory and honour to your name.

I desire to be a Priest in this company and pledge to lead this company for Christ to the best of my ability. I will do everything in my capacity as < your role >, to honour you in all the practices and dealings of < Company. >

I now dedicate < Company >, and all its assets to you for the advancement of your Kingdom.

Help me God, to carry out all that I pledge to do, in Jesus' name. Amen.

Signed by Signed by   ....
(Name) (Date)
Witnessed by: ....
(Name) (Date)

God's part

As the lead partner, He gives us the necessary resources to develop the work.

He gives financial resources. "He called ten of his servants and gave them ten minas. 'Put this money to work,' he said, 'until I come back.'" (Luke 19:13) A mina was a Greek monetary unit worth one hundred denarii or about four months' wages for an average worker based on a six-day work week. Quite a large sum was given to invest - something like € 80.000 today!

He gives us skills, intelligence and know-how to carry

out the work He has for us to do. "Then Moses said to the people of Israel, "See, the LORD has called by name Bezalel the son of Uri, son of Hur, of the tribe of Judah; and he has filled him with the Spirit of God, with skill, with intelligence, with knowledge, and with all craftsmanship, to devise artistic designs, to work in gold and silver and bronze, in cutting stones for setting, and in carving wood, for work in every skilled craft. And he has inspired him to teach, both him and Oholiab the son of Ahisamach of the tribe of Dan. He has filled them with skill to do every sort of work done by an engraver or by a designer or by an embroiderer in blue and purple and scarlet yarns and fine twined linen, or by a weaver—by any sort of workman or skilled designer." (Exodus 35:30-35)

As lead partner, He gives wisdom to make good decisions. "If any of you lacks wisdom, you should ask God, who gives generously to all without finding fault, and it will be given to you." (James 1:5)

As lead partner, he instructs and guides. "I will instruct you and teach you in the way you should go; I will counsel you with my loving eye on you. Do not be like the horse or the mule, which have no understanding but must be controlled by bit and bridle or they will not come to you." (Psalm 32:8)

As lead partner, God is ultimately in control of every event. "We adore you as being in control of everything" (1 Chronicles 29:11, TLB). "The Lord does whatever pleases him, in the heavens and on the earth" (Psalm 135:6). And in the book of Daniel, King Nebuchadnezzar stated: "I honoured and glorified him who lives forever. His dominion is an eternal dominion; his kingdom endures from generation to generation. All the peoples of the earth are regarded as nothing. He does as he pleases with the powers of heaven and the peoples of the earth. No one can hold back his hand or say to him: 'What have you done?'" (Daniel 4:34-35).

As lead partner, God even uses seemingly devastating circumstances for ultimate good in the lives of the godly, whatever the circumstances. "We know that in all things God works for the good of those who love him, who have been called according to his purpose" (Romans 8:28).

A major aspect of God's part is that he gets involved in pruning or cutting down in order to cause more fruit to appear.

Jesus spoke explicitly about the fact that we cannot bear spiritual fruit unless we stay connected to the vine. "I am the vine; you are the branches. If a man remains in me and I in him, he will bear much fruit; apart from me you can do nothing" (John 15:5).

Jesus said, "I am the true vine, and my Father is the gardener. He cuts off every branch in me that bears no fruit, while every branch that does bear fruit, he prunes so that it will be even more fruitful" (John 15:1–2).

Spiritual blessing from God often begins with pruning. I see many entrepreneurs come to believe in the Lord. They express enthusiasm and gratitude for their new life with the Lord and expect God to bless them right from the start! They forget that the pruning comes before the process of growth. I have often heard young Christian businessmen say, "I thought everything would be going my way now that I've become a Christian, but now I encounter more problems than before."

This observation is correct, and it is just what God wants. The owner of the vineyard has to work hard, tidying up, removing rocks, breaking the hard soil, weeding, and clipping the branches before any fruit appears. Sometimes a whole company has to be cleared away if the roots are rotten.

My mind goes back to a businessman who used to do interior decorating for brothels and other property connected to the underworld in Amsterdam. After his conversion he refused to continue this work, even being threatened to do so at gunpoint! His business quickly went under, but he himself started growing in his faith and trusting God for a new business. He started another company, again in interior decorating, but this time built on a better foundation and with a different customer base. He never went back to his old market.

My part

My role in the new partnership is to walk daily with the Lord and work with him in His mission. Jesus' mission was explained so succinctly in Mark 10:45. "For even the Son of Man did not come to be served, but to serve, and to give his life as a ransom for many." Jesus came to serve people and to set them free - to enable them to be all that they can become and enjoy all the Lord created.
Here are some examples of my part.

We are to work conscientiously with Christ and for Christ. "Whatever you do, work heartily, as for the Lord and not for men, knowing that from the Lord you will receive the inheritance as your reward. You are serving the Lord Christ." (Colossians 3:23,24)

We are to follow the instructions God gives for our work. The Bible gives us complete insight into how to work as a believer. "All Scripture is God-breathed and is useful for teaching, rebuking, correcting and training in righteousness, so that the man of God may be thoroughly equipped for every good work." (2 Timothy 3:16)

We are to be trustworthy in handling the money entrusted to us faithfully, according to the owner's wishes.

"Whoever can be trusted with very little can also be trusted with much, and whoever is dishonest with very little will also be dishonest with much. So if you have not been trustworthy in handling worldly wealth, who will trust you with true riches? And if you have not been trustworthy with someone else's property, who will give you property of your own?" Luke 16:10-12

We are to work hard at completing our assignments. "Whatever your hand finds to do, do it with all your might" (Ecclesiastes 9:10)

My part is to be careful from whom I receive counsel and advice, and whom to associate with.

"Blessed is the man who does not walk in the counsel of the wicked or stand in the way of sinners or sit in the seat of mockers. But his delight is in the law of the Lord, and on his law he meditates day and night. He is like a tree planted by the streams of water, which yields its fruit in season and whose leaf does not wither. Whatever he does prospers" (Psalm 1:1-3)

This reminds me of some very good Irish advice at a renowned horse-racing event when a friend was asked, "Whatever is that old nag doing in this race?" The answer was, "I know he has no chance of winning, but the association will do him good."

During my career in business, I have found that associating with other Christian businesspeople has done me a lot of good! It helps to give a Biblical perspective on business instead of a worldly perspective.

An example of a disciple in the workplace

When the process of building the tabernacle was started, specific instructions were given to Moses. One of his key workers was Bezalel.

The Lord said to Moses, "'See, I have chosen Bezalel son of Uri, the son of Hur, of the tribe of Judah, and I have filled him with the Spirit of God, with wisdom, with understanding, with knowledge and with all kinds of skills — to make artistic designs for work in gold, silver and bronze, to cut and set stones, to work in wood, and to engage in all kinds of crafts. " (Exodus 31:2-5)

This gives us a picture of how God works together with us in partnership to make something beautiful. Bezalel is a prototype of a Christian worker.

He has been chosen, by name. His name means, 'in the shadow of God." Working in partnership with God means to work in his presence, under his shadow, under his influence. Maybe he learned his trade in Egypt as a slave working on palaces and tombs of Egyptian Pharaohs. Now, however, he has been released from slavery and set free to serve God with his skills and talents. The tabernacle is a symbol of God's presence in the wilderness. People were invited there to experience God's holiness and his glory. The tabernacle, built with the finest materials, was to reflect the beauty of God's character.

Bezalel was filled with the Holy Spirit, as we are as believers. This is the first person in the Bible we read about being filled with the Spirit. He and we are filled with the Spirit and empowered for special work which he has prepared. For us.

"For we are God's handiwork, created in Christ Jesus to do good works, which God prepared in advance for us to do." (Ephesians 2:10)

- He was given wisdom, insight, knowledge, creativity and the ability to implement the tasks needed. Wisdom is knowing how and knowing when to do things. Understanding gives us insight into how things work, what is available and who we need to help us. Knowledge helps us to solve the many problems which crop up.
- He was given the creative force of the Spirit to make plans, designs and implement them. He has the ability to get things done, to be productive. He does in small ways what God did in Genesis 1.
- He was also given the resources needed for the assignments he was asked to take on.
- He was given some help, as we read in Exodus 35:6. "Moreover, I have appointed Oholiab son of Ahisamak, of the tribe of Dan, to help him. Also, I have given ability to all the skilled workers to make everything I have commanded you."

We see here a transformation of Bezalel's work from slavery to freedom. Freedom to use his gifts and talents for the glory of God, that He may be known to the nations as the only God with Israel. That He would be with us. He takes us from meaninglessness … to meaningful use of all that God gives you.

Chapter 4: Managing Wealth

At the end of their desert wanderings, Israel stops at the Jordan River, prior to entering the Promised Land.

The book of Deuteronomy is a collection of stories and laws written by Moses as they pause before entering the land. The Jordan River is representative of a spiritual boundary. In the scarcity of the desert, Israel learned to trust God daily through the precious gift of manna (Exodus 16). It fell in abundance for the community so that no one went hungry. But it could not be hoarded by individuals out of fear or faithlessness or the desire to profit. Nothing fell on the Sabbath. A day of rest after gathering, working and earning was at the heart of God's economic purpose for His people.

But now the scarcity is behind them and across the river lies a land overflowing with milk and honey. The paradox of a Promised Land given to all God's people is that some will be prosperous, and others will be in debt, even in slavery. The story poses a vital question to us in today's affluent culture: can a contented, prosperous people remain faithful in a place of plenty?

Building capital in God's economy begins with God's provision. When Moses led the people of Israel to the Promised Land, he warned them not to forget God, who had brought them out of bondage, out of the land of 'not enough', through the desert of 'just enough' and into the land of 'more than enough'. Abundance is promised. Unfortunately, many Christians live in the land of 'just enough' and have not travelled any further!

It is my prayer that we can enjoy 'the Promised Land,' of abundance. God's economy is not determined by scarcity but by abundance.

However, in 'The Promised Land,' 'giants' were present. Moses sent out twelve people to explore the land. Ten came back and, "they told him, and said: "We went to the land where you sent us. It truly flows with milk and honey, and this is its fruit. Nevertheless, the people who dwell in the land are strong; the cities are fortified and very large; moreover we saw the descendants of Anak there. The Amalekites dwell in the land of the South; the Hittites, the Jebusites, and the Amorites dwell in the mountains; and the Canaanites dwell by the sea and along the banks of the Jordan."

Then Caleb quieted the people before Moses, and said, "Let us go up at once and take possession, for we are well able to overcome it."

But the men who had gone up with him said, "We are not able to go up against the people, for they are stronger than we." And they gave the children of Israel a bad report of the land which they had spied out, saying, "The land through which we have gone as spies is a land that devours its inhabitants, and all the people whom we saw in it are men of great stature. There we saw the giants (the descendants of Anak came from the giants); and we were like grasshoppers in our own sight, and so we were in their sight."" (From

Numbers 13:27-33)

Two men, Joshua and Caleb, came back with the challenge; "If the LORD delights in us, then He will bring us into this land and give it to us, a land which flows with milk and honey.' Only do not rebel against the LORD, nor fear the people of the land, for they are our bread; their protection has departed from them, and the LORD is with us. Do not fear them." (Numbers 14:9)

The 'Giants' are food … that is what we live on … difficulties are opportunities!

The Lord's promise to make the people of Israel wealthy in their new land is found in this key verse.

"You shall remember the LORD your God, for it is he who gives you power to get wealth, that he may confirm his covenant that he swore to your fathers, as it is this day…." (Deuteronomy 8:17,18)

The key words here are "wealth" and "covenant". We can acquire wealth to build a business, because God wants to work out His covenant - His alliance with mankind in practical terms.

Covenant

The Bible text indicates the purpose for acquiring wealth - 'so that God may confirm His covenant'.

The Hebrew word for covenant is 'berîyt.' Strong's concordance of the Bible describes the original meaning our word covenant:14 'a compact (because made by passing between pieces of flesh): — confederacy, covenant, league. Alliance, pledge between men, treaty.
Man to man - constitution, ordinance agreement, pledge. Alliance of friendship, alliance of marriage.

Between God and man – alliance of friendship, covenant (a divine ordinance with signs or pledges)

In the Old Testament, five main dimensions of His

covenant with mankind are expressed.

The covenant with Adam that embraces the cultivation and preservation of creation. The covenant with Noah was an unconditional covenant between God and Noah and with humanity in general. This indicates the value of each individual and the protection of life.

The covenant with Abraham with a promise of blessed generations and a land of its own.

A covenant with Moses, promising prosperity if obedience.

Later, God made a covenant with David, confirming his kingship and his line. Christians now know that these expressions of God's covenant with mankind receive their fulfilment in Christ, with the New Covenant. The New Covenant in Christ is the release and fulfilment of the Old Testament covenants.

The covenant with Adam, which was subject to sin, could thus be freed from the yoke of sin, and so our work no longer has to involve 'thorns, thistles and sweaty foreheads'. We may use the resources of the earth, but not abuse them.

The covenant with Noah can be realised in giving value and dignity to people and protecting life.

The covenant with Abraham becomes a reality in recruiting people who share your mission and immediately have an area, or market, to work in.

The covenant with Moses becomes a reality in following God's Word, which leads to well-being and prosperity for people.

The covenant with David takes shape in a servant, spiritual leadership and in necessary successors.

Wealth

What is wealth? For entrepreneurs, this is usually expressed as capital in financial terms. The meaning in the Bible text shows that wealth is much broader. It is the competency, capacity, energy, and strength to get something done, to be able to accomplish something. It includes everything that can be used by an enterprise to realise its purpose.

The Hebrew word for wealth is 'hayil.' Strong's concordance explains this wide-reaching meaning:15 '...a force, whether of men, means or other resources; an army, wealth, virtue, valour, strength: ability, activity, army, band of men (soldiers), company, (great) forces, goods, host, might, power, riches, strength, strong, substance, valiant, virtuous, war, worthy.'

In discussing wealth, we will use the 'capital' or it's synonym 'assets.'   There are five dimensions of Biblical capital. Spiritual capital, relational capital, productive capital, physical capital and finally, financial capital.   These form a network of interdependent qualities that give the enterprise strength to achieve its God-given goals.

In order to 'keep the covenant', we need to invest our acquired capital.

When Jesus speaks of discipleship, he always speaks through the lens of investment, looking at what we might gain. He promises people that what initially looks and feels like a sacrifice will eventually pay off, which is the same as making a good investment.

"The kingdom of heaven is like a treasure hidden in a field, which a man finds and hides; and in his joy over it he goes and sells all that he has and buys the field. Likewise, the kingdom of heaven is like a merchant who sought beautiful pearls. When he had found a precious pearl, he went and sold all that he had, and bought it. "(Matthew 13:44,45)

"Whoever has given up houses or brothers or sisters or father or mother or children or fields for my name's sake, will receive back many times more and inherit eternal life. " (Matthew 19:29)

Acquiring capital

God promises us the capital to multiply our resources. God promised that obedience to His commandments and rules would make the children of Israel rich. "Take care lest you forget the LORD your God by not keeping his commandments and his rules and his statutes, which I command you today, lest, when you have eaten and are full and have built good houses and live in them, and when your herds and flocks multiply and your silver and gold is multiplied and all that you have is multiplied, then your heart be lifted up, and you forget the LORD your God, who brought you out of the land of Egypt, out of the house of slavery." (Deuteronomy 8:11-14)

But above all, they should not forget the source of their wealth during all this prosperity. "Beware lest you say in your heart, 'My power and the might of my hand have gotten me this wealth.'
You shall remember the LORD your God, for it is he who gives you power to get wealth, that he may confirm his covenant that he swore to your fathers, as it is this day. And if you forget the LORD your God and go after other gods and serve them and worship them, I solemnly warn you today that you shall surely perish. Like the nations that the LORD makes to perish before you, so shall you perish, because you would not obey the voice of the LORD your God." (Deuteronomy 8:17-19)

Some Questions To Consider

1. Peter gave a definition of financial discipleship. It means to:

    a. honour God as the owner of everything, (Lordship)

    b. be good stewards of His resources, (Stewardship)

    c. share what we are entrusted with for His purposes. (Generosity) and

    d. pass on what we have learned to others. (Multiplication)

In your workplace, what does it mean, to …

    a. a. honour God as Lord of your life and Owner of everything you have under your control.

    b. Be a steward of the Lord's resources

    c. Share what we control for His goals

    d. Pass on what we have learned to others

2. On page 13, Peter gives seven reasons why finances are a key to discipleship.

- Which resonates the most with you, and why?

3. Chapter 2 describes some common financial problems in your workplace which explain the reason for following Biblical principles in handling finances at work.

- Which have you experienced in your workplace? How were these problems handled?

4. Chapter 3 describes how financial management is a partnership between the Lord and I. Each has a specific role to play.

    a. Describe in your own words what God's part is in financial management.

    b. Describe in your own words what your part is in financial management.

5. Chapter 4 talks about acquiring wealth and for what purpose

    a. Describe in your own words what wealth actually is

    b.. God said that the purpose of wealth, is 'to establish His covenant.' What does this mean to you?

    c. What are the conditions the Lord sets to enjoy His promise to create wealth?

Part Two: The Creation, Fall & Redemption of Finance

In this part, we will consider the foundations of finance from a spiritual perspective. We believe that God is in control of everything and that finance is part of His order for mankind. Mankind, however, fell into sin and still fall short of God's original design. Thankfully, we are invited to be a part of the redemption of the original order. We will look at several functions of finance in an organisation; what was originally intended, how these can be corrupted and how they can be redeemed.

At the end of Part Two, you can look at some questions which you can consider concerning God's best practices, how these are often missing in the workplace and how the best practices can be re-applied.

Chapter 1: Creation, Fall & Redemption

Dr. Tim Keller said that the basis of the Christian worldview can be described by the process of human history. 16 "The Bible reveals the history of the world in four stages: (1) creation by God, (2) fall into sin, (3) redemption through Christ, and (4) final restoration by Christ—a millennium of peace and prosperity.

Creation, fall, redemption, and restoration are not just periods in time; they are also different aspects of present reality.

We can look at anything (tangible or intangible) in this world, and we immediately know four things about it:
- First, it is part of God's good creation, yet,
- second, it is fallen and affected by sin—distorted somehow, broken, falling short of its original purpose. But,
- third, it is being, and can be, redeemed -

utilised as it was originally envisaged. And
- fourth, one day when Christ physically returns, all creation will be restored to its original form in wholeness, beauty, and glory."

We will look at some aspects of why money is beneficial to the way in which God has designed us later in this chapter.

However, as we are fallen, the way we use money has also fallen. Many times, it is used to manipulate and enslave people. Our transactions can be affected by stealing, cheating, lying and deceit. Financial dealings can be redeemed through honesty, justice, grace, and generosity.

Ultimately, when Christ terns to redeem creation, all transactions will be conducted in righteousness and justice in the coming millennial kingdom, characterised by peace and prosperity.

In thinking about the foundations of finance, we need to recognise God's sovereignty over everything, including finance. We should not relegate some parts of God's creation to the secular but consider all of creation as being under His power and authority, and that He gives us an invitation to redemption, and to return to His Kingdom.

I do not believe God created a particular system of finance, but he created the necessity for finance.

People are created in ways that give finance a unique role to play in fulfilling God's purposes for us. God chose to enable finance in order to help facilitate the expression of our identity in the material world the Lord created.

The Lord gave us resources to discover, develop and use. He instructs us to work with these resources and be productive. The fruits of our labour are to be shared by all for mutual well-being. Finance facilitates these opportunities to fulfil our identity as productive workers, making good use of the resources He gives us and sharing the bountiful fruits of our labour.

In other words, finance turns the conditions of human existence into opportunities to bring glory to God, to serve as stewards of creation, and to care for each other with justice and love.

When thinking about God's purpose for the finance part of His creation, we need to understand how finance can be used to love our neighbour and promote just dealings. If financial transactions do not bring justice and love, then we are not using the finance part of God's creation as He intended.

There are eight aspects of creation of human beings which form the necessity of finance to facilitate these expressions of who we are. I am grateful to Leonard van Dusen of Calvin College, and his contribution to the Theology of Work project for permission to use these eight points. [17]

We are placed in time and space.

God created a world in a limited space and with a limited time span. Humans were also created in that space in time which is limited. In God's creation there are days, seasons, generations, and lifetimes. The Bible admonishes us to use our allocated time and tells us that will be held accountable for how we use our time. Of course, time cannot be managed, but we can manage what activities we choose to do in the time available. Resources need to be allocated to these activities. Allocating these resources among people across different time periods, and across different spaces is the foundation of finance. Financial resources are needed for a few days because of production or shipping time, maybe a few months due to seasonal business, a half year due to a growing season, for several years to develop and new product, or for decades to build a factory or buy a house, or for most of a working lifetime to accumulate retirement savings. In a world where people's needs, opportunities, and available resources vary over time, finance is the primary means of matching resources to needs across time.

We are created as social beings

Human beings are created to be social and to live in community, and we have a desire to be with other people. As God put it, "It is not good that the man should be alone" (Genesis 2:18). Moreover, we are created in God's image, and the Holy Trinity existing in perfect unity is a model of a loving community. Finance is a social and a relational activity in that it facilitates sharing and the exchange of resources between people.

We are not all created the same

God created people with a wide variety of talents and skills so that they should work together. They also have very different needs and desires. In addition, since we were not all born at the same time, human society has a rich variety of ages and life stages. Some people are young and not yet able to provide their own food and shelter, others are just beginning to be able to do so and need education and training. Others are in their prime productive years and have resources in excess of their current needs, and still others are older and need help in supporting themselves or need to draw on resources accumulated during their earlier years.

Finance is very helpful because at any given time some people will have excess resources to utilise, while others will have needs or opportunities to use resources beyond that which they currently possess. For example, some of us will want to borrow money to pursue a business opportunity or build infrastructure to fulfil some unmet need in society. Others will be savers at some periods of their lives and will be able to lend to meet that borrowing need.

We are agents

People were created to act on others' behalf, to be stewards or agents. A prime example is that we can act on God's behalf to steward his creation, His mysteries and the gospel. (1 Corinthians 4:1,2) We have many Biblical examples. God called Joseph to act as a steward for both Potiphar and Pharaoh. Jesus' parable of the talents illustrates that we are his stewards and will be held accountable for acting as he would want us to. (Matthew 25:14-30)

When we act as agents or stewards on behalf of others, we need finance. Executives act as agents for the shareholders of a corporation. Mutual fund managers act on behalf of investors to decide which stocks or bonds in which to invest. Lawyers apply their expertise to serve their clients' interests in financial transactions. An entire branch of finance literature is devoted to better understanding the many agency relationships in finance. Finance is needed because God created people with an ability to act on behalf of others.

We make promises

God is a God of promises and covenants. The biblical narrative is a story of God's promises kept. Humans are created in his image, and thus we have biblical accounts of humans making promises to each other. The story of Ruth hinges on promises between people of different nationalities, for example (Ruth 1:16 -18). Paul references human promises in Galatians 3:15. Humans are created to be able to make and keep promises to each other.

Every financial instrument is a promise between two or more parties and would not be possible if promises were not part of God's creation. A mortgage loan is a promise to pay a certain amount each month. A share of stock is a promise for a portion of future dividends and a right to elect board members. In modern finance some of our promises tend to get quite complicated and detailed so it has become common practice to write them down. However, these written contracts simply reflect our created ability to make and keep promises. This ability is so central to finance that the Bible teaches us to not overpromise in our finances. (Proverbs 22:26-27).

We don't know it all

Humanity does not know everything, and individually each of us knows only a tiny fraction of what can be known. God created each of us with our own unique mind which takes in, processes, and remembers things differently from anyone else. Human endeavour depends on each of us using our individual knowledge for mutual benefit, rather than on each of us learning everything needed for success.

Limited knowledge, and 'asymmetric information,' (where one party has more information than another,) is mediated by financial markets. This means that when a loan is entered into, the borrower has more information about his or her ability to repay than does the lender. Finance is built on two obligations which turn asymmetric information from a hindrance into an opportunity. First, we use promises to convey our certainty about information we possess that other parties do not. My promise to repay the mortgage, under penalty of losing the house, gives you the confidence to deposit money in the bank that funds the mortgage, even though you do not know what my future earnings will be. Secondly, we prohibit falsifying information in financial transactions. If your investment documents tell me that there is a $3 billion market for products like yours, this information must be accurate. Because of this, we can make use of information provided by others, even if we do not have personal knowledge of its accuracy.

We don't know the future

God does not reveal to us in detail what the future may bring. Because people are created with free will, and we do not know what their decisions will be, we do not know what the future holds (Ecclesiastes 8:7). Therefore every decision we take involves risk at some level.

This risk has a profound impact on financial decisions. Most financial instruments and the pricing of those instruments reflect this uncertainty. Loans get turned down due to uncertainty or are priced higher to compensate for the percentage expected to fail. Share prices rise and fall due to uncertainty. Debt contracts have reporting and collateral provisions because of uncertainty. Financial markets are greatly complicated by uncertainty, but also have a greater potential benefit to society due to the ability of risk to be managed and re-allocated via finance.

We have a free will

God took a risk by creating us with free will, giving us resources to use and setting us free to make independent decisions. Money is a facilitator of our will. It enables us to transform our decisions into reality.

Created in his image, we too are risk-takers. Trust is a risk-willing decision we take. We do not know if the trust will be repaid by a virtuous partner. This relationship between trust and risk can be limited in commercial transactions by placing boundaries on our financial obligations.

The dark side

An element of our Biblical worldview is described by what Paul wrote about creation in Colossians 1:16,17. "For by him all things were created, in heaven and on earth, visible and invisible, whether thrones or dominions or rulers or authorities—all things were created through him and for him. And he is before all things, and in him all things hold together."

God created systems whereby society is held together and can function. These systems are governed, as we would say today, 'in the cloud,' unseen powers which are ultimately under the control of Christ. However, these powers at some stage in time, rebelled against Christ and set up to use these systems for their own ends.

Ezekiel described the fall of such a power in chapter 28. "You were an anointed guardian cherub. I placed you; you were on the holy mountain of God; in the midst of the stones of fire you walked. You were blameless in your ways from the day you were created, till unrighteousness was found in you. In the abundance of your trade, you were filled with violence in your midst, and you sinned..." (verses14-16)
Then Ezekiel goes on to describe this fallen power; "By the multitude of your iniquities, in the unrighteousness of your trade you profaned your sanctuaries." (verse18) In the unrighteous way in which this power organised trade and exchange, the godly nature of trade and exchange was profaned, it lost its godly characteristics and became 'of the world' and not as Christ intended.

For a full description of the fall of the power behind trade and exchange, you could read chapters 26-28 of Ezekiel, in which he uses the multinational trading nation of Tyre to illustrate how Tyre allowed itself to be influenced by the fallen powers.

Business is still influenced by these fallen powers today. Paul warned believers in Ephesus, which was a large city full of financially successful businesses, but also full of dark arts. "For we do not wrestle against flesh and blood, but against the rulers, against the authorities, against the cosmic powers over this present darkness, against the spiritual forces of evil in the heavenly places." (Ephesians 6:12)

These powers are, praise God, still under some restraint in order to prevent our lives falling completely into chaos and evil. He defeated these powers at the cross, and now they are granted only limited powers to deceive and to tempt; "by cancelling the record of debt (*of sin)* that stood against us with its legal demands. This he set aside, nailing it to the cross. He disarmed the rulers and authorities and put them to open shame, by triumphing over them in him." (Colossians 2:14,15)

On a more personal level Jesus set some conditions for serving God with money in his sermon, given to many people to describe the Kingdom of God. "No one can serve two masters, for either he will hate the one and love the other, or he will be devoted to the one and despise the other. You cannot serve God and money. (Matthew 6:24)
Jesus used the Aramaic word for money in his sermon, which is '*mammon*'. He was unmasking a spiritual power behind money which is actively tempting us to serve money instead of God. When we serve God and look to His interests, this spiritual power of money can be neutralised.

In the following pages, we will look at 10 aspects of organisational finance from the viewpoint of creation, fall and redemption.

We will discuss what God has to say about each aspect and how he designed these functions of organisational finance. Then, we will observe how each function is being influenced by 'the dark side.' Lastly, we will look at how these functions can be redeemed to, once again, reflect God's original design, and how we can imitate God as His agents in the workplace.

Chapter 2: Ownership

At creation the Creator gave humanity a commission to care for the world and its resources. (Genesis 1:28–29) Man and woman were made in the image of God and they were commanded to work with creation, and to exercise dominion over it.

The concept of dominion should not be understood in terms of forceful domination or aggressive abuse. Dominion is the power and authority which God has given us to work the earth and care for it; We are to use all available resources and to bring all processes under control for the benefit of people so that they can flourish. Dominion reflects an aspect of God's nature which we call 'sovereignty.'

We imitate God by exercising dominion over creation. The idea of holding a right to property is an important biblical idea. The eighth commandment says, "You shall not steal." (Exodus 20:15) The Old Testament also condemns those who would move 'property markers' and stealing.[18]

New Testament teaches to respect what belongs to others.[19] This teaching gives us a basis for the legal and economic principle of property rights and is a tool God gives us to exercise dominion. The command, 'You shall not steal,' makes no sense if we don't have a mutual understanding of what is mine and what is yours.

An important aspect of 'ownership' is that you only have access to and control over property for a certain period of time and under certain conditions. In that sense, there is no such thing as absolute ownership. You only have control over a company as long as it is sufficiently financially healthy, or until it transitions into new management through takeover or inheritance. If you don't pay your mortgage, debts, or taxes, you will soon see how fleeting ownership is!

One of the first things law school teaches, is that legally, you do not own property, but it is a bundle of rights that can be split among many individuals or entities. These include rights to use, exclude others from using, and to transfer property to someone else. When a law is passed to protect private property, it in fact protects individual *control* over property.

The term 'private property' is used by many as a fundamental concept of economics. However, property is almost never private. It is used by many people. The office coffee machine is the property of the company, but it is certainly not private, only for the exclusive use of the owner. If it was, there would be a revolution in the office!

We imitate the nature of God when we take good, productive care of a business, an asset or money entrusted to us, until it outlives its usefulness or is passed on. When we take good care of our resources, we imitate God who is talking care of the whole universe.

We imitate God by taking care of His creation, protecting

the environment, and not exhausting the resources available but developing sustainable processes.

The dark side

Ownership gives plenty of opportunity to misuse the resources we have at our disposal.

- We can pollute the environment.
- We can use resources wastefully, on self-indulgent spending.
- We can misuse the power which ownership gives us to misuse people and manipulate them for profit maximisation.
- We can use resources to advance our own pride at all we have accumulated.
- We could become greedy and selfishly accumulate property for its own sake.
- We could develop a spirit of independence, resting on that we have been able to achieve.
- Property rights may be hoarded and guarded, stopping people from sharing in the ownership of property.

Personal, independent ownership can lead to pain and hurt when things go wrong. "There is a grievous evil that I have seen under the sun: riches were kept by their owner to his hurt, and those riches were lost in a bad venture. And he is father of a son, but he has nothing in his hand." (Ecclesiastes 5:13,13)

A.W. Tozer describes the problem of ownership as a 'monstrous substitution.' He said, "There is within the human heart, a tough, fibrous root of fallen life whose nature is to possess, always to possess. It covets things with a deep and fierce passion. Things have become necessary to us, a development never originally intended. God's gifts now take the place of God, and the whole course of nature is upset by this monstrous substitution."[20]

Redeeming ownership

Property rights are both a gift and a power God has entrusted to us as stewards. We imitate God when we accept our role as stewards, as managers of Gods possessions and use resources for His purposes.

Stewardship is a way of working which encompasses the responsible planning and management of resources. Stewardship principles can be applied across a wide range of human activities, such as the caring for the environment and nature, economics, health, property, information, theology, gifts and talents.
Stewardship implies accountability, which stimulates a more responsible use of the assets under management. Stewardship implies sustainability, which contributes to the effective and durable use of resources.

We can identify four major principles governing stewardship.

1. The principle of delegated control.
The concept of stewardship begins with creation. "The earth is the Lord's, and all its fullness, the world and those who dwell therein." (Psalm 24:1)
Whatever God makes, He owns.

Stewardship is a foundational way in which we can imitate God's sovereignty and authority. When we have money or talents, or position, we can imitate God by taking care of these and using them for good.
When we take use and care for our resources, we imitate

God's character using His wisdom, knowledge, creativity, love, kindness, fairness, justice, freedom, and joy!

God has the ultimate ownership of all we 'possess.' He has given these things to us in trust and expects us to manage them according to His ways. God put Adam in the Garden to work it and to take care of it. Man was created to work, and that work is the stewardship of all of the resources God has placed at his disposal.

This is the fundamental principle of biblical stewardship. God owns everything, and we are simply managers or administrators acting on his behalf.

Stewardship is an expression of our obedience to His ways. Stewardship is the commitment of all we have under our control to God's service and utilising this under His guidance.

2. The principle of responsibility.

We have to be responsible for what we actually do with the resources we have been entrusted with. Instead of holding tightly to our rights, we are to hold strongly to our responsibilities. We are called as God's stewards to manage that which belongs to God and are responsible to manage his resources efficiently and effectively, according to his desires and purposes. To act responsibly implies we have to be 'response-able,' that is, always ready to give an account of what we have done with the resources.

3. The principle of accountability.

We will all will be called to give an account for how we have managed what the Master has given us.

Like the servants in the Parable of the Talents, we will be called to give an account of how we have administered everything we have been given; our time, money, abilities, information, wisdom, relationships, and authority.

We will all give account to the rightful Owner as to how

well we managed the things He has entrusted to us. For we must all appear before the judgment seat of Christ, so that each one may receive what is due for what he has done in the body, whether good or evil." (2x Corinthians 5:10)

4. The principle of reward.

Christ's evaluation of our work will have consequences. We want to please Christ, so that these consequences will be beneficial to us.

Paul writes, "Whatever you do, work at it with all your heart, as working for the Lord, not for men, since you know that you will receive an inheritance from the Lord as a reward. It is the Lord Christ you are serving." (Colossians 3:23,24)

The Bible teaches that faithful stewards who manage the master's resources faithfully, in accordance with His will, can expect to be rewarded incompletely in this life, and fully in the next. When asked, "What would you like to hear when you come to stand before Jesus?" The most-often heard reply is "Well done, good and faithful servant." I certainly long to hear the Master say, "Well done, good and faithful servant! You have been faithful with a few things; I will put you in charge of many things. Come and share your master's happiness!" (Matthew 25:21)

A steward's primary goal is to be "found faithful" by his master. (1 Corinthians 4:2) He proves himself faithful by wisely using the master's resources to accomplish the tasks delegated to him. Those resources include not only money but time, gifting, relationships, employment, and life opportunities.

Jesus commands, "Do not lay up for yourselves treasures on earth, where moth and rust destroy and where thieves break in and steal but lay up for yourselves treasures in heaven." (Mathew 6:19,20a) These treasures are the rewards for faithful stewardship.

Randy Alcorn said, "Seen from this perspective, stewardship isn't a narrow subcategory of the Christian life. On the contrary, stewardship is the Christian life." [21]

He aligns with a similar quote by John Piper, "The issue of money and lifestyle is not a side issue in the Bible. The credibility of Christ in the world hangs on it." [22]

Chapter 3: Money

Money facilitates human activity in which we allocate or exchange resources between parties with respect to time and space. Finance helps people who want to borrow some resources in a particular time period by entering into arrangements with people who have more resources than they currently need.

Money is a facilitating agent to help get things done. Money enables us to be productive and to enjoy the fruits of that productivity. If there was no money, we would have to barter, and most of us have so little to barter, to trade with.

Money is something that everyone is willing to trade with and use to facilitate exchange of goods and services. Money helps to place a value on what I have, and thereby facilitates exchange. It is also a store of value, until it is needed.

Money makes voluntary exchange more extensive and efficient.

Money also facilitates borrowing and lending. The borrower is willing to pay extra, in the form of interest or a premium, to gain access to the resources, and the lender wants to make a profit or return in the future from releasing access to the resources. The lender serves the borrower by providing resources when the borrower needs it, while the borrower benefits the lender with future profit.

We can imitate God as financial disciples by being fair, just, and honest in our transactions, as the Lord is always fair and honest with us. "Does God pervert justice? Or does the Almighty pervert the right?" (Job 8:3)

We can imitate God by being truthful and keeping our promises, reflecting God's nature. "God is not man, that he should lie, or a son of man, that he should change his mind. Has he said, and will he not do it? Or has he spoken, and will he not fulfil it?" (Numbers 23:19)

We can imitate God by being faithful to our commitments, as He is. "if we are faithless, he remains faithful—for he cannot deny himself." (2 Timothy 2:13)

We can imitate God by being generous, as He is generous. "He who did not spare his own Son but gave him up for us all, how will he not also with him graciously give us all things?" (Romans 8:32)

I believe God uses money in three ways. God uses money as a tool, a test and a testimony.

As a tool to assess our capacity to use money well. In Matthew 25, God gives large amounts of money to three stewards who are expected to do business with what they have been entrusted with. To those who used the money well, according to the master's wishes, the master complemented them. The reward of good stewardship was more stewardship! "Well done, good and faithful servant. You have been faithful over a little; I will set you over much." (Matthew 25:23) The reward was also the 'the joy of the master'.

As a test to assess our faithfulness in using the money in

the right way. Especially with the little we are entrusted with. "One who is faithful in a very little is also faithful in much, and one who is dishonest in a very little is also dishonest in much." (Luke 16:10) The extent to which we will be trusted with what Jesus called "the true riches" is to a large extent determined by how well we use the money entrusted to us. "If then you have not been faithful in the unrighteous wealth, who will entrust to you the true riches?" (Luke 16:11)

And the extent to which we will be given more money to manage is also determined by how faithful we are in managing Gods money as a trusted steward. "And

if you have not been faithful in that which is another's, who will give you that which is your own?" (Luke 16: 12)

As a testimony to those around us as they see God working through our lives as we trust Him in all our financial decisions. It is a great testimony to our Lord when we live a life of contentment and thankfulness despite the difficult circumstances, and when we are generous and sharing what we have to alleviate needs of others.

The Dark Side - Finance and the Fall

Until Christ's redemption of creation is fully accomplished, we live in a world shaped by both the good of all God has created and the evil of the Fall. Our ability to be faithful stewards has been seriously damaged by sin. Ur capacity to show justice and love through our financial transactions has been seriously limited.

Handling money is not just a technical exercise of adding, subtracting, percentages but it is essentially a spiritual discipline, because we handle something which is inherently neutral, but which has a driving force behind it.

Jesus gave money a name, *mammon,* and personified it, giving it 'god-like' characteristics. Mammon is an Aramaic word that usually means 'money' and also can mean 'wealth.'   Neither the Jews nor Gentiles of His day knew a god by this name. He could so easily have said,' you cannot serve both God and Caesar,' or 'you cannot serve both God and Baal, or Apollo, or Zeus.'

Jesus did not use a pagan god to show that you must choose between the true God and a false god. Jesus gives this term a force and a precision that it did not have in its milieu.

This personification and deification of money also means that it is something that claims divinity. What Jesus is revealing, is that money is a power. The Bible speaks a lot about the struggle with 'the powers' of this world.' When Paul was in Ephesus, he warned the people in Ephesus, a city with great wealth, about the power of money and its effect on their life. "For we do not wrestle against flesh and blood, but against the rulers, against the authorities, against the cosmic powers over this present darkness, against the spiritual forces of evil in the heavenly places."   (Ephesians 6:12)

Mammon is such a power. It strives to give spiritual meaning and direction. It is not neutral; it directs, moves, and controls our hearts and minds. This power competes for our allegiance to God. "No servant can serve two masters; for either he will hate the one and love the other, or else he will be loyal to the one and despise the other. You cannot serve God and mammon." (Matthew 6:24) Jesus calls for a choice. Who will we serve, God or mammon?

Paul Tillich wrote, "These powers drive nations and individuals into insoluble conflicts, internal and external; into arrogance and insanity, into revolt and despair, into inhumanity and self-destruction. Each of us is involved in these conflicts and driven to a greater or lesser degree by these forces. The personal life of each of us is in some way determined by them. No security is guaranteed to anyone; no house, no work, no friend, no family, no country anywhere in the world is safe, no plans are certain of fulfilment, all hopes are threatened. This is not a new state of things in human history. But what is new is that during a few years of comparative safety, we had forgotten that this is the true state of things." [23]

For every visible front of a person's life, there is an invisible background that profoundly influences us. We do our best, to serve God and our neighbour, to do a
good day's work, but we often find ourselves frustrated with 'the system' of fallen powers which resist us. The systemic evil of the fallen powers makes life tough for us.
We constantly experience unjust and unloving systems of business and finance, principles of conformity and social patterns, that marginalise the life of faith or positively oppose it.

Prof. Jacques Ellul, wrote in his wonderful book 'Money & Power;'[24] "The Hebrew word for money,' *kesef*,' comes from a verb meaning 'to desire, to languish after something.' This implies that from the very beginning, when the Hebrew language was being formed, the spiritual character of money as well as its power was already stressed. This relation between money and desire shows that lust for money dwells in us."

The key to overcoming the fallen power behind money is given by Jesus when He stated, "You cannot love both God and mammon." The key is to love God and obey all he is telling us about managing money in His Word.

Redeeming Money

Money can be redeemed when we live and work out of Christ's work on the cross which broke the power of money. He did this, "by cancelling the record of debt that stood against us with its legal demands. This he set aside, nailing it to the cross. He disarmed the rulers and authorities and put them to open shame, by triumphing over them in him." (Colossians 2:15) Jesus broke the power of money by allowing himself to be sold as a slave for money and to be bought by the Pharisees, thereby breaking the power of buying and selling to set us free!

When we consciously transfer all that we have under our control into God's hands, and accept His ownership of all things, we take mammon off the throne; we take away his leadership and influence over the finances we control. We then manage money, instead of money managing us.

Money can be redeemed by taking away its sacred, holy powers.   Then the work of mammon, the spoiler, will be negated by giving the first and best part of all income and moving money into God's economy!

"Bring the full tithe into the storehouse, that there may be food in my house. And thereby put me to the test, says the Lord of hosts, if I will not open the windows of heaven for you and pour down for you a blessing until there is no more need. I will rebuke the devourer for you, so that it will not destroy the fruits of your soil, and your vine in the field shall not fail to bear, says the Lord of hosts." (Malachi 3:10,11) Giving the tithe breaks the power of money, and 'the devourer', mammon, can no longer spoil the work of our hands.

The powers that use money cannot take that most uneconomical of all transactions - giving. In the world economy, money is use for taking, for bargaining, for manipulating, but not for giving. This is exactly why giving has such ability to defeat the powers of money.

We redeem money through prayer. We must pray for our businesses, organisations, and government institutions. Karl Barth once said that "to clasp the hands in prayer is the beginning of an uprising against the disorder of the world."[25]
"Submit yourselves therefore to God. Resist the devil, and he will flee from you. Draw near to God, and He will draw near to you." (James 4:7,8)

Money is redeemed when we choose people over money. Jesus told a parable about a business manager who was called to give account of wasting the owner's assets. (Luke 16:1-8) the owner praised the manager for solving the problem with some innovative steps of reducing the debts of his customers. "The master commended the dishonest manager for his shrewdness." (v8) Then Jesus explained the meaning of the parable in verse 9. "And I tell you, make friends for yourselves by means of unrighteous wealth, so that when it fails, they may receive you into the eternal dwellings." The praise was for using money to reduce the debt burden of debtors and establishing such relationships which lead to spiritual benefits.

When Jesus was travelling on the other side of the Sea of Galilee, He came across two violent men who were possessed by demons. The demons cried out, "If you drive us out, send us into the herd of pigs." He said to them, "Go!" So they came out and went into the pigs, and the whole herd rushed down the steep bank into the lake and died in the water. Those tending the pigs ran off, went into the town and reported all this, including what had happened to the demon-possessed men. Then the whole town went out to meet Jesus. And when they saw Him, they pleaded with Him to leave their region." (Matthew 8:3-34)
The people of that town valued their pigs more than

people.

What would it look like for finance to participate in God's redemption of the world? God's redeeming grace, operating through people in financial transactions, can redeem finance's ability to honour God, foster good stewardship, and show justice and love to people.

What would your workplace look like if God's financial principles were faithfully carried out? Just think a moment … and imagine …

Chapter 4: Buying and Selling

Buying and selling are basic to human existence and to achieve anything beyond mere subsistence living. Without this function, no individual or family could ever provide for their needs beyond a very minimum. We could only produce a very simple range of food and clothing. Enjoying the full range of what resources God has provided, means we have to exchange goods with one another in a buying and selling function.

Through this function, we can imitate God by practising honesty and fairness, keeping our promises and freedom of choice.

Through this function, we can serve our neighbour and do benefit others. I have a stock of products, which do not do anything, but represent a store of value. If I sell you a my product for €10, I can buy something I need and you get something useful! That is worth €10 to you. We are both better off than before and we have realised value for each other.

Commercial transactions provide opportunities for personal interaction, relating to one another, with opportunities to demonstrate love and grace.

I remember talking to the sales director of Samsonite, manufacturers of luggage. He explained how he handles a case in which he could not reach agreement with a customer over terms to make a deal. He carries a plastic disk in his pocket, with the inscription, "Do as you would be done by." In effect, he is asking the customer, "if you were in my position, what would you consider a fair deal?" He says that this opens up negotiations because the other party starts thinking differently.

The statement he put in front of his customer is a paraphrase on Jesus' words, "So whatever you wish that others would do to you, do also to them, for this is the Law and the Prophets." (Matthew 7:12) This known as 'The Golden Rule.' (In the marketplace today, however, the Golden Rule often means, 'he who has the gold, makes the rules!)

This reciprocal 'doing good' to one another is an important aspect of transactional relationships which will be long-lasting and mutually profitable.

When buying and selling we demonstrate inter-dependence and love, which imitates the nature of the trinity in which the members demonstrate perfect love and inter-dependency.

The Bible recognises this essential transactional relationship, expecting that people will buy and sell without disadvantaging the other in any way. "And if you make a sale to your neighbour or buy from your neighbour, you shall not wrong one another." (Leviticus 25:15)

The dark side

Commercial transactions are, however, influenced by the

fruits of sin. Rather than seeking the good of another, transactions can be saturated with greed, manipulation, cheating, dishonesty, lies, misrepresentations and poor quality products or services.

I remember taking a friend to a lunch at Schiphol, Amsterdam airport to hear the testimony of Bob Hage, vice-president of McDonnell Douglas, the aircraft manufacturer. Bob was due to tell guests why he is a Christian and what difference this meant to him as a business- and family man. My friend looked around the room to see who else was present. He pointed out someone else to me, whom he knew as a regular church attendee, and stated, "If he's a Christian, I'm not interested." He was referring to the way this person conducted his business, which was not so attractive.

The dark side of buying and selling is no stranger to Christians. Many break their promises to pay on time, conveniently 'forget' their promises and commitments; betray a partner's trust, or deliver sub-standard work. Such problems can destroy our testimony quickly.

Powerful customers can exert unnecessary price pressure on suppliers, causing such problems as oppression, product quality, overwork, stress, and loss of freedom.

Buying and selling are good and necessary but can be fraught with potential danger.

Redeeming transactions

The Bible teaches us that the world economy of buying and selling is going to get such a strong grip that there will be a time in which we will not get a share in economic traffic unless we participate in a perverse trading system (with Babylon as a symbol) that will eventually fall. We are already living at the beginning of this process!

The Bible says that there will come a time when it will be made impossible to buy and sell unless we carry 'the brand of the Beast'; and in that time, even the souls of people will be sold! (Revelation 13:17 & 18:13)

The mechanism of buying and selling, if not curbed by God's economy, can lead to manipulation and ultimately to enslavery of people. Think only of modern slavery in the factories of Bangladesh and the sale of young girls into prostitution, and we realise these times are not far off!

The buying and selling relationship has another characteristic, it profanes that which is sacred. That is, it violates, desecrates, or debases the Kingdom activities of giving and receiving.

The prophecy of Ezekiel about Tyre, probably the world's first multinational trading empire, strongly and clearly reveals that commerce ends up by 'profaning what is sacred.' After having described at length Tyre's imports and exports, all its trade which leads to power (chapters 26-27), Ezekiel concludes: "By the multitude of your iniquities, in the unrighteousness of your trade you profaned your sanctuaries."(Ezekiel 28:18) Profane means to treat something good with abuse, in an unworthy or unholy way.

This does not mean that the system of buying and selling is wrong. It has been controlled by the fact that it is a contractual system that is subject to certain accepted standards and legal rules. We, as citizens and strangers, can engage in buying and selling based on these accepted standards and laws in such a contractual system with respect for its rules, laws and with care for the interests of others.

Jesus Himself was involved in a buying-selling transaction. He was told for thirty pieces of silver by Judas, which was the going price for a slave in Jerusalem's markets. He was bought for thirty pieces of silver by the Pharisees, who wanted Jesus under their control, so that the Roman authorities could nee manipulated to kill Jesus.

Prof. Jacques Ellul, says in his book 'Money and Power,' "The selling of Jesus, first foreshadowed by the story of Joseph sold by his brothers, then by Amos (2:6), shows the constancy of the selling relationship and carries it's meaning to the absolute. This sale defines all selling. They sold the Righteous. This act, which is our act, is reflected in each selling relationship. Now all money affairs are characterised by the fact that Jesus became the object of a money relationship. And because the Son of God was thus turned into merchandise, all subordination of humankind to money is intolerable."[26]

We don't need to be educated about buying and selling, but rather we need salvation from it! Through the contractual system of buying and selling, Mammon ultimately wants to enslave us; the Holy Spirit wants to set us free!

Jesus allowed Himself to be subject to the perverted buying and selling mechanism, so that through His death and resurrection we could be set free from the fallen nature of commercial transactions. In place of buying and selling, He introduced the Kingdom transaction of giving and receiving.

Our commercial transactions can be redeemed when we apply the Kingdom economic principles of giving and receiving. Remember you do not work for a living, but for a giving …

The concept of giving and receiving in the economy of the Kingdom has liberated me from the pressures of selling.

I have always worked in commercial ventures and, surprisingly, found the sales process always very stressful. So, how does this work? I am called to give to my customers the best of my talents, experience, skills, gifts and serve them to meet their needs and to help them achieve their goals. In return, I will receive out of God's provision, what I need for the continuation of the business. Remember, we work for 'Almighty & Co.' The Owner, God, instructs companies or people to pay me … if they don't … they will have to deal with God!

Giving & receiving leads to healthy and strong reciprocal relationships.

In his classic book, 'the 7 Habits of Highly Successful People,'[27] Steven Covey talks about negotiations in Habit 4. In this, he describes the Win/Win strategy, which is a frame of mind and heart which seeks mutual benefit in all agreements or interactions.

With a win/win solution, all parties feel good about the decision and thereby are committed to the deal. Win/win sees life as a cooperative, not a competitive arena. It is based on the premise that there is enough for everyone and that success is not achieved at the other's expense.

We imitate God when we works with a covenantal system, which gives an extra dimension to the contractual system. For example, learning to give, looking for the best interests for the other person, doing good, considering the other person more excellent than yourself, walking the extra mile are actions which introduce people into the economy of God's kingdom.

Chapter 5: Credit

Borrowing and lending are fundamentally good and offer opportunities to imitate God as financial disciples. The Bible does not prohibit lending or borrowing, but it does give some boundary rules and warns about the dangers.

By extending credit, we imitate God by demonstrating grace and justice. "It is well with the man who deals generously and lends; who conducts his affairs with justice." (Psalm 112:5) The psalmist describes a righters person as one who is, "ever lending generously" (Psalm 37:26)

By extending credit, we can imitate God by protecting the poor and the integrity of the family home. "When you make your neighbour a loan of any sort, you shall not go into his house to collect his pledge. You shall stand outside, and the man to whom you make the loan shall bring the pledge out to you. And if he is a poor man, you shall not sleep in his pledge. You shall restore to him the pledge as the sun sets, that he may sleep in his cloak and bless you. And it shall be righteousness for you before the LORD your God." (Deuteronomy 24:10)

We imitate the nature of God in lending to the poor without acting as a moneylender, and not burdening the poor with excessive terms. "If you lend money to any of my people with you who is poor, you shall not be like a moneylender to him, and you shall not exact interest from him." (Exod. 22:25)

We can imitate God by providing a temporary credit to help people work their way out of poverty—a loan that helps them to utilise their gifts and talents and serve their community. Microfinance institutions offer short-term business loans to suitable entrepreneurs to help them climb out of poverty.

I remember listening to a presentation from two Ethiopian women at a European Economic Forum gathering in Amsterdam. They told of receiving two very small loans which were used to buy two sewing machines for women in the village. Some of the proceeds of selling the clothes they made was re-invested in the cooperative movement in the village. Years later, that cooperative had an investment fund of approaching a million dollars! This self-sustaining movement is bringing many people out of poverty.

The Bible also gives some warnings when borrowing money. "Owe no one anything, except to love each other, for the one who loves another has fulfilled the law." (Romans 13:8) This is not a prohibition to borrow, but an admonition to pay what is due, fully and on time. When we do this, we demonstrate love to our creditors. I have been in business for over 40 years, and I really love those customers who pay on time! It is a joy to do business with them! On the other hand, if a customer does not pay up on time, relations get strained, and I have to watch that I don't start hating them! Having worked hard to timely deliver a good product, and the customer does not pay, is one of the most joy-killing aspects of business.

When you take credit from a supplier, you promise to pay a certain amount in a certain time. If you do not keep this promise, you find yourself in a lie, a deceitful situation which is ungodly. The psalmist says not paying back is 'wicked.' "The wicked borrows but does not pay back, but the righteous is generous and gives." (Psalm 37;21)
If you do keep all accounts up to date, paying what is due, you don't morally owe anything. All obligations are being met.
However, when problems crop up, you could get into a situation, in which you must default.. This is morally wrong and this opens the door for ungodly actions or attitudes.

A further warning which the Bible gives is that borrowing can remove your freedom. "The rich rules over the poor, and the borrower is the slave of the lender." (Proverbs 22;7)
When we borrow, and cannot pay back on time, the creditors have first call on our financial priorities. Those who have experienced this, suffer the pressure of banks, creditors, and even collection agencies. We run the risk of losing freedom, because we are not free to use our money according to our own priorities – our creditors determine what our priorities should be. .

We borrow expecting that in the future, we will be able to repay. The future is very uncertain and we do n to know if we can pay back from future earnings.
"Be not one of those who give pledges, who put up security for debts. If you have nothing with which to pay, why should your bed be taken from under you? Do not move the ancient landmark that your fathers have set." (Proverbs

80

22:26-28)

I had the privilege to speak with Dr. Frits Philips son of the founder of the global electronics concern. He explained to a group of businesspeople that Philips had a policy of not borrowing more than 20% of the total assets of the company. This was to keep a high degree of solvency, the ability to meet financial obligations at all times. This is a 'ancient landmark' which we could do well to set ourselves. If times are tough, we can then sell some assets to meet our debts, and not get 'indebted.'

The Bible also warns against giving a guarantee for debts. The proverb says that if the time comes when you have to cover the loan from personal means, you could out your family at risk. "Be not one of those who give pledges, who put up security for debts.
If you have nothing with which to pay, why should your bed be taken from under you? Do not move the ancient landmark that your fathers have set." (Proverbs 22:27)

Borrowing and lending facilitates the multiplication of goods and services which we can enjoy.
In borrowing and lending we can imitate God in our trustworthiness, honesty, timeliness, and faithfulness.

The dark side of borrowing

The origins of debt go all the way back to the fall of man in the Garden of Eden. When Eve was tempted by the serpent and had to give an account of what she had done, she explained, "the serpent deceived me … then I ate." (Genesis 3:13)
This word 'deceived' in Hebrew comes from a root 'nasha' which represents a homonym = a word having different meanings - to deceive, and also to lend at interest.

This Hebrew word is strongly linked to the Hebrew word *'nashak'* which means 'to strike with a sting!' This appears for instance in Habakkuk 2:7. "Will not your creditors (*nashak*) suddenly arise?   Will they not wake up and make you tremble? Then you will become their victim."

This tells us that lending at interest is at its root a deceit, tempting people into bondage. Just like the serpent tempted Eve into a bargain of debt which she could never, ever repay. Borrowing money is almost like opening a Pandora's Box, because we never know what is going to happen next! Opening Pandora's Box refers to getting into a situation over which you have no control over the outcome.

According to the old Greek story, the first woman, Pandora, was sent as a curse to Zeus and his men and was given a present upon her marriage. She was to be the first of a long one of women, destined to live with mortal men as companions only in times of plenty, and desert them when times became difficult! (Does this sound like a bank?). Her wedding present was a box that she was told never to open. However, her curiosity got the better of her (like eating forbidden fruit). Eight demons were set free in the world. The first seven represented the seven deadly sins, and the last, which she managed to capture, was hope.

The Czech professor, Dr. Tomas Sedlacek said during a speech at a conference I helped organise in Berlin, "Eve and Adam grab the opportunity and eat the fruit. The original sin has the character of excessive, unnecessary consumption. It is not of a sexual nature. A desire for something she doesn't need is awakened in Eve. The living conditions in paradise were complete, and yet everything God had given the two wasn't enough. In this sense, greed isn't just at the birthplace of theoretical economics, but also at the beginning of our history. Greed is the beginning of everything."

One of the deadly sins is greed. Tim Keller says, "Jesus

warns people far more often about greed than about sex, yet almost no one thinks they are guilty of it." [28]

There are a number of practical problems associated with debt.

1. Debt encourages you to spend more than you can afford.
There's something about debt that tempts you to keep spending even when you can't afford the payments. Part of the temptation of debt is getting an emotional high from buying new things now, without having to deal with the pain of parting with the money now. It can almost feel like you're getting something for nothing. However, the debt payments catch up with you, and it doesn't feel that good anymore.

2. Debt costs money
Debt appears to set you free when you're swiping your card or signing loan documents, but it's not freedom at all. You will be paying a premium for the debt you create. The higher the interest rate, the more you'll end up paying. When consolidating loans, a short-term relief may be gained, but you'll end up paying much more in the long term.

3. Debt borrows from future income
When taking on debt you are borrowing from the money you hope to earn in the future. You may end up paying for something which is already used or has lost in value.

5. Debt can keep you from reaching your financial goals
Debt payments limit the amount of money you have to spend on other things.
Credit card, car, and student loan debt are all taken into consideration and could negatively affect your capacity to get a mortgage. Debt payments also take away capacity to

build a retirement fund, or even to be able to be generous.

7. Debt can lead to health problems.
Worry and anxiety about making payments often accompany debt. Stress caused by debt can lead to mild or even severe health problems including ulcers, migraines, depression, and heart issues.

8. Debt can hurt relationships
Debt puts unnecessary pressure on a family's finances and creates a lack of financial security for the family. It is a major cause of   arguments between marriage partners, which can easily lead to marriage breakdown.
Unpaid loans can seriously damage relationships with friends. When asked for a loan, a friend of mine answered, "What do you want most? Money or a friend?"

Redeeming credit

Our word 'credit' comes from the Latin '*credere*,' which means 'to trust, entrust, believe.'   If we are to demonstrate our faith and belief in God, and imitate God with regard to credit, then we should start with His standards.
This was given in Deuteronomy 28 in which Moses communicates benefits of demonstrating obedience to God's will.   Concerning credit, he says., "And all these blessings shall come upon you and overtake you, if you obey the voice of the Lord your God ... The Lord will open to you his good treasury, the heavens, to give the rain to your land in its season and to bless all the work of your hands. And you shall lend to many nations, but you shall not borrow." (Deuteronomy 28:2 & 12)

The norm for God's people was that they should be blessed with assets which they could lend out and not have to borrow. I know many businesses which have started and continued with zero debt. Israel was to be a special people which would bless nations, so that they may know who God is.

I believe that the norm for Christians is to develop their assets so that we can give freely to those in need and be generous, asking nothing in return.

"Give to everyone who begs from you, and from one who takes away your goods do not demand them back. And as you wish that others would do to you, do so to them.

And if you lend to those from whom you expect to receive, what credit is that to you? But love your enemies, and do good, and lend, expecting nothing in return, and your reward will be great, and you will be sons of the Most High, for he is kind to the ungrateful and the evil. Be merciful, even as your Father is merciful." (From Luke 6:30-36)

Showing grace by not only forgiving a debt, but even 'going the extra mile,' is redeemed credit in action.

Victor Hugo's story *Les Misérables* gives an inspiring example of grace.

Jean Valjean, imprisoned for stealing a loaf of bread to feed his starving family, was released on parole. He moved about the country trying to find work but was discriminated everywhere as an ex-con. One day he was given lodging for a night by a bishop.

Instead of showing gratitude for the bishop's kindness, he rewarded him by stealing some silver candlesticks and running away. He was apprehended by the police. Valjean said that the bishop had given him the silver. The police did not believe Valjean and took him back to the bishop's house to verify his story.

The bishop, showing grace to Valjean, said that he had, indeed, given the candlesticks to Valjean. Moreover, he also gave Valjean some more silver which Valjean had forgotten to take with him. What a wonderful example of grace – turning the other cheek when you have been slapped in the face. This act of mercy was used by the bishop to try to teach Valjean a life lesson. He says to Valjean, "Jean Valjean, my brother, you no longer belong to evil, but to good. It is your soul that I buy from you; I withdraw it from black thoughts and the spirit of perdition, and I give it to God".[29]

Valjean, could not understand this radical act of grace. He resolved to give up his old ways and to follow what the bishop's told him to "use this precious silver to become an honest man." Valjean was redeemed by grace and entered a new reality. This is the purpose of using money in a way that doesn't make earthly economic sense: to introduce people into God's world of grace. Is it possible to "buy back" someone's soul through acts of selfless kindness? That is exactly what Jesus did for you and me.

Chapter 6: Prices

Prices reflect the relative scarcity and value of our resources.

From a marketing viewpoint, a right price can be seen at the junction between the supply and demand. When a rise in the price of a product makes it more expensive for buyers to purchase it, they normally choose to buy less of the product. For the buyer, there is a negative relationship between the price and quantity demanded. This is the Law of Demand. For sellers, a rise in the price of a product makes some more willing to supply more of it. For the summer there is a positive relationship between the price and the quantity they produce. This is the Law of Supply. The intersection off the supply and demand curves gives us a market price. Both sides of the exchange will benefit, as long as the prices between maximum the customer is willing to pay and the minimum price the seller is willing to sell.

You could say that all market prices are just because they are reached in cooperation between buyer and seller.

From a stewardship viewpoint, the resources God has provided for us have multiple uses. Prices help us make good decisions about how, where and when to use our resources. Good stewardship is to make sure that your labour and the value added to goods you manage reach the highest level of value to customers- easier said than done, because customers are always looking for reduced prices as much as possible.

When confronted with a price for a product, we have three choices. We can pay the price and buy the product if we really need it. If we think the price does not bring us the expected value, we can leave it and not pay the price. Prices reflect the value consumers think the products are worth. There is a third way.

Prof. Alex Tabarrok coined the phrase, "A price is a signal wrapped up in an incentive."[30] When a price rises, this gives a signal that something needs changing. For instance, before the oil crisis in the 70-ies, oil was used to heat glasshouses to grow roses. When the oil became too expensive to grow roses at the right price, manufacturers turned to growing roses in Kenya where there was an abundance of warmth. New logistic systems for the roses were developed, and roses could be sold to the consumer for a lower price. This freed up scarce oil for products with a greater added value.

Professor Tabarrok added, "if it had been invented, the price system would be one of the most amazing creations of the human mind, but like language it wasn't invented and it worked long before anyone had any understanding of its principles." He quoted the Nobel Prize winning economist Vernon Smith, who put it; as "the pricing system is a scientific mystery as deeply fundamental, and inspiring is that of the expanding universe or the forces that bind matter."

The price system is, therefore, not a creation of the human mind, but has been created by God to facilitate the cooperation of producers and consumers in the marketplace.

The dark side.

Suppliers must indicate the price of a product clearly, so that the potential user can easily decide if it is value to him or her and can easily compare similar offerings.

I once booked a flight to Spain and discovered at the very end of the booking process, the price had doubled due to several surcharges which had not been mentioned at any time during the booking. The service department said that the price mentioned as 'indicative.' Of course, a supplier can offer additional services, but these must be mentioned from the start!

Quoting prices which do not include all relevant costs are unfair I recently downloaded an app, which as 'free' until I realised that it was useless without paying for the 'pro' version.

During the Covid-19 pandemic, social media was hot with stories of hand sanitiser being sold online many times more that it's pre-crisis price. This is a practice called 'price gouging' - selling at a price considered to be unfair or making unethical use of a scarcity of needed products.

Predatory pricing, which is focussed on putting a competitor out of business is part of the dark side or of pricing. A bus business in the UK competed for a franchise after deregulation, by undercutting prices considerably.[31] Later, the CEO of the firm, acknowledged that the negative impact of his strategy far exceeded any financial gains.

As I am writing, we are going through a period of high inflation. Supermarket prices have increased by 20%. I was surprised when I opened a packet of pancakes to discover there were only six instead of the usual eight- of course, for the same price! The economists call this 'shrinkflation.' This is used as a way to combat inflation, but it is deceptive. Manufacturers should be transparent and honest at what they are selling for the same price. Shrinkflation is a form of lying.

Redeeming prices

We can imitate God by offering prices which are as fair as possible. One company says, 'our prices are as low as we can go to stay in business." That seems a good motto for the Christian who wants to reflect the character of God.

We need to remain committed to God's standards and not this of the world. It is His reputation which is at stake, as we carry the name of Christ into the marketplace. "A good name is to be chosen rather than great riches, and favour is better than silver or gold." (Proverbs 22:1)

Offering full and transparent disclosure about our pricing is a reflection of the truthfulness and love of God. "Rather, speaking the truth in love, we are to grow up in every way into him who is the head, into Christ…" (Ephesians 4:15)

Bill English writes, "Healthy economic transactions are fully voluntary and meet the needs and interests of both parties. This doesn't mean we do away with self-interest; it merely means we disclose enough information to make the transaction truly voluntary. In addition, we do not use deception in our negotiations. Voluntary transactions must have a proper disclosure of truthful information flowing both ways. To do otherwise is sin."[32]

I wanted to buy some colourful cloth for my wife after a conference in Guatemala. My friend, a local businessman, told me never to pay the asking price and expect to haggle and negotiate. "They always inflate the price, expecting haggling." In many societies around the works, bargaining is a common practice, the merchant often accepting a fraction of the original offer. I do not believe this is a practice a Christian should adopt. When a seller makes a habit of price bargaining, it gets really difficult to determine if he or she is telling the truth. We want people to deal with us in the same way as we would want to deal with others. The Biblical principle is, "Do to others whatever you would like them to do to you. This is the essence of all that is taught in the law and the prophets." (Matthew 7:12 NLT)

The truth is the ultimate standard. "The integrity of the upright guides them, but the crookedness of the treacherous destroys them." (Proverbs 11:3)
I

Chapter 7: Productivity

Productivity is essential for a company's profitability and its ability to flourish and grow. It is a measure of economic or business performance that indicates how efficiently people and organisations convert inputs, such as labour and capital, into outputs, such as goods or services.

The productivity of a company's workforce plays a key role in its profitability and competitiveness. When productivity levels increase, you can generally expect to generate better profits without adding more workers.

While different types of work can be more or less productive, productivity of any kind is obviously better than the alternative. However, we cannot *focus solely on efficiency*; this would certainly negatively affect other virtues. However, without efficiency and productivity, tasks are not accomplished, and we make no progress.

Some may question the purpose of productivity.

Why should we work to produce more, more and more? Wayne Grudem explained, "Increasing the production of goods and services is not morally evil – and it's not morally neutral – rather, it's fundamentally good and pleasing to God. It's part of his purpose in putting human beings on the Earth. When we create something, productivity creates value in the world that didn't exist before. Therefore, productivity imitates God in his creativity…God's wisdom led him to create us with a need and a desire for material things."[33]

God put Adam in the garden of Eden to '"work it and keep it." (Genesis 2:15) This was before sin came into Adam's life to distort the results of his work. How mandate to Adam and his descendants was given previously in Genesis 1:28. "And God blessed them. And God said to them, "Be fruitful and multiply and fill the earth and subdue it, and have dominion over the fish of the sea and over the birds of the heavens and over every living thing that moves on the earth."

The Hebrew word used for 'subdue' is '*kabash*,' which means to 'bring under your control for your benefit.' God intended Adam to develop the earth's resources, and bring them under his control, to use them to benefit himself and others. He could take the earth's resources of minerals, plants, and animals, and harness their properties. He could take animals and make shelter for them, raise food for them and produce agricultural products needed to sustain life. For this production, tools would be needed, which meant development of metal products, housing needed which needed wood working resources.

If the human race was to multiply, then these processes would be to be done on larger scale and efficiently to sustain larger populations.

The Hebrew word used for work in Genesis 2:15 is *'avodah.'* This word is used in the Bible many times and has three meanings which complement one another beautifully. The first meaning is simply hard work, such as when the children of Israel had to work hard making bricks as slaves in Egypt. "So they ruthlessly made the people of Israel work *(avodah)* as slaves and made their lives bitter with hard service, in mortar and brick, and in all kinds of work in the field. In all their work they ruthlessly made them work as slaves." (Exodus 1:13,14) The second meaning is service. "Furthermore, whom should I serve? Should I not serve *(avodah)* the son? Just as I served your father, so I will serve you." (2 Samuel 16:19)

The third meaning is to worship. When Moses Speke to the Pharaoh of Egypt demanding release for the people of Israel, he gave as a reason, "This is what the LORD says: Let my people go, so that they may worship *(avodah)* me." (Exodus 8:1)

For the believer, work, service, and worship and one and the same. When we work, we serve and worship God. "Whatever you do, work heartily, as for the Lord and not for men." (Colossians 3:23) In the process of productive work, we are given opportunities to serve our neighbour, demonstrating love and understanding their needs.

In working for the new employer, "Almighty & Co.," we work above all to serve others and glorify God - not for a wage. Remember, the Lord is our Employer and will provide all we need ... and more!

Christians at work in the factories, offices, schools, marketplaces of today live in glasshouses. If people know we are Christians, we will be watched to see if our standards line up with the name we carry into our work - Christ Himself. Jesus says that we are 'the light of the world,' and tells us to "let your light shine before others, so that they may see your good works and give glory to your Father who is in heaven." (Matthew 5:16)

The desire to increase or multiply the fruits of our labour is, in this way, certainly not materialistic. Growth in productivity reflects God-given desires to help people, solve problems, achieve goals. It represents the need to execute faithful stewardship to work all the resources of creation, to take care of them and enjoy their fruits.

The dark side of productivity

Adam failed to obey God and followed the temptation of the evil one to know good and evil. The results of this knowledge of good and evil, can be seen in the dark side of productivity. After Adam disobeyed God, we see that work (which is still intrinsically good) comes with fundamentally two dangers, which we can read in Genesis 3:17-19.

The first is personal pain, the 'sweat on your face,' the physical burden and stress which work can entail.

The second is futility, the apparent meaninglessness of work, the 'thorns and thistles' which often accompany our work. Thorns are a symbol of sorrow and hardship, experienced as disappointment or failure. Thistles symbolise adversity and pain— like weeds that choke out what we are trying to grow in our business or personal life.

Our "thorns and thistles" may appear as conflicts, lack of resources and cooperation, dishonesty or mistakes that interfere with our productivity.

We are confronted daily with the sobering reality that our work, the people we work with and our workplaces are not as God originally designed. Tim Keller in his book, 'Every Good Endeavour,' put it simply. "Sin runs through the heart of every worker and the culture of every enterprise."[34] Work is not the problem; sin is the problem.

We see the dark side of productivity in the manipulation of workers to overwork to produce the required results. In the oppression of workers to produce with little reward. In cutting corners regarding safety and healthy working conditions. In abusing animals, wasting resources, and polluting our environment.

Often workers are merely a means of production. One businessman told me, "Our metal fabrication industry is so cutthroat. Workers are asked to constantly do unpaid overtime, and maximum output is demanded. They're just a production factor."

Doug Sherman and Howard Hendricks, in their book, 'Your Work Matters to God,' gives us hope: "Work is not our enemy. Sin is our enemy - and only Christ is adequate to deal with sin. His strategy for dealing with sin, however, is never to remove us from the jungle, but instead to make us adequate to live in the jungle. . . Sin may make the work world a jungle. But we must never forget that Christ is the Lion of Judah, the King of the jungle!"[35]

Redeeming Productivity - Good works

The Good News is that work can be redeemed. Remember that Christ wore a crown of thorns on His head at His crucifixion. He carried the sin, the pain, the futility of our life to the cross so that we may be set free from the curse which followed sin.

God created us to work and prepared good works for us to do. "For we are his workmanship, created in Christ Jesus for good works, which God prepared beforehand, that we should walk in them." (Ephesians 2:10) The Greek word for 'good,' is '*agathos*,' which means, according to the Greek Lexicon; 'of good constitution or useful, pleasant, agreeable, joyful, excellent, distinguished, upright and honourable.'

Paul's ceaseless prayer for the Colossians runs; "that you may be filled with the knowledge of his will in all spiritual wisdom and understanding, so as to walk in a manner worthy of the Lord, fully pleasing to him: bearing fruit in every good (*agathos*) work and increasing in the knowledge of God." (Colossians 1:9,10)

It is 'good' in the sense of being beneficial to others. We imitate God when we carry our productive work to the benefit of others.

One of my mentors in my career, the Austrian Dr. Siegfried Buchholz, who was managing director of the chemical giant BASF in Austria, wanted me. "People do not pay for your talents or skills. They do not pay you for the quality of your products. They pay you for how useful you are in helping them achieve their goals."

Redeemed work gives meaning to all kinds of work. Martin Luther King Jr. is quoted as saying, "If a man is called to be a street sweeper, he should sweep streets even as Michelangelo painted, or Beethoven composed music, or Shakespeare wrote poetry. He should sweep streets so well that all the hosts of heaven and earth will pause to say, here lived a great street sweeper who did his job well." [36]

Redeemed productivity enables us to use all tour resources, time, talent and treasures, for the benefit of others and to the glory of God, with creativity and competence.

It involves knowing how to get things done as efficiently and effectively as possible, so that we can serve others in a way that really benefits them without burdening co-workers in the process through overloaded, overwhelming, and too-demanding productivity systems.

Chapter 8: Profit

Profit is simply an excess of income over expenses. It is a return on the investment made in a business after all expenses are accounted for.

We can imitate God as financial disciples at work, when we contribute to the profitability of the organisation we work for. The multiplying effect of planted seeds and animals which the Lord has given us to steward, demonstrates that God wants us to increase in wealth.

Profitability, increasing wealth and material gain are natural outcomes of a just exchange of goods and services, in well-functioning relationships. Profit, or increase, comes when we utilise creation in harmony with God's ways. We can glorify God by efficient and effective management of what He has placed under our control and stewardship by enlarging these resources to serve more people.

Making a profit, imitates God by sound planning, wisdom, problem solving, and special skills.

Writer Jim Collins in 'Good to Great' writes, "Profitability is a necessary condition for existence and a means to more important ends, but it is not the end in itself … Profit is like oxygen, food, water, and blood for the body; they are not the point of life, but without them, there is no life."[37]

Profit must never be the goal of a business. The goal is to seek the rule of God's Kingdom and his way of doing things. "But seek first the kingdom of God and his righteousness, and all these things will be added to you." (Matthew 6:33) God affirmed this when reminding Israel in Deuteronomy 8:18 that wealth was not gained by their own efforts but by His grace, acting to realise His covenant. "But you shall remember the LORD your God, for it is He who is giving you power to make wealth, that He may confirm His covenant which He swore to your fathers, as it is this day." (Deuteronomy 8:18)

There is a persistent concept that the ultimate purpose of a business is to maximise profit for the company's investors. Maximising profit is not a purpose. Profit it is an outcome of a well-run business. The best way to maximise profits over the long term is to *not* make them the primary goal.

The profit motive should never be a guiding factor in business. Business is fundamentally intended to serve – to deliver goods and services which contribute to the wellbeing and development of the community - and to worship God, which involves obeying His commands.

Profit is a result of productive work and the productive utilisation of capital resources, ensuring that the return on invested capital exceeds the cost of capital. If the firm fails to do so, it is actually destroying wealth in society -- finances, intellect, and human. It is reflection on the good use I have made of the resources given to m manage and that through creativity, wisdom, effective working and problem-solving I have been able to add value for customers. Without profit there can be no re-investment in the business, causing growth to be limited or even business decline.

When investing capital to start and run a business, it is only fair to expect a good return, as the investor has lost the opportunity to invest the money elsewhere, such as an interest bearing deposit in a bank. He or she deserves to be compensated for this 'opportunity cost.' It is only fair to consider the risks the investor takes. There is a genuine chance that some of that money will be lost.

Companies need a purpose that transcends making money; a spiritual and moral call to serve all who have an interest in the business and to sustain the business in the long-term.

The dark side

The influential economist Milton Friedman famously stated that "the social responsibility of business is to increase its profits." [38]
The pursuit of profit as an end in itself can be dangerous and harmful. Jesus warned us; "For what will it profit a man if he gains the whole world and forfeits his soul? Or what shall a man give in return for his soul?" (Matthew 16:26)

Jesus posed this very penetrating question which I wrestled with for a few years as a long CEO. At age 30, I was managing director of a chemical company, and achieving all I wanted. However, God was not in the equation. I was pursuing profit and wealth, but these can with a high cost, which I did not realise at the time. My health was deteriorating due to work and financial pressures. I was hospitalised for some weeks. My relationship with my wife and children was suffering, due to much travel and giving priority to business instead of family. My spiritual life was almost non-existent. I remember distinctly sitting in church one morning, and the only think I could think about was how rot pay the bills the next day. I was losing my soul. Fortunately, I joined a group of Christian businesspeople who helped me get my priorities re-aligned with God and my family.

I realised at that time when you pursue profit, you are loving money which opens the door to all kinds of evil. Paul's words to Timothy became reality. "But those who desire to be rich fall into temptation, into a snare, into many senseless and harmful desires that plunge people into ruin and destruction. For the love of money is a root of all kinds of evils. It is through this craving that some have wandered away from the faith and pierced themselves with many pangs." (1 Timothy 6:9,10)

The dark side of profit could reveal itself by promoting inequality through over-priced products; through cost-cutting of workers' wages or removing production to low-invoice areas; through over-production and excessive pollution.

The dark side emerges where competition is purposefully stifled or neutralised.

The dark side occurs when too much emphasis is put on profits and not enough emphasis on other aspects of the business such as customer service, employee care and well-being, and other goals and product quality.

An easy way to reach profit maximisation in financial management is to cut employee training or the research and development budget. While this will reduce operating expenses, and maximise short-term profits, it will not help the company reach any long-term sustainable goals and could even potentially harm employees.

Redeeming profit

A year and a half before the 2008 financial crisis shook the foundations of the global economy, a major shareholder of the Mars Corporation, a large multinational company, asked the CEO a question that shocked his fellow shareholders.

'What is the right level of profit for the corporation?'

The obvious answer was surely *'As much as possible!'* However, this lead the leadership of Mars to question whether his company was taking too much profit. This led to the development of a policy called" Economics of Mutuality."

I was privileged to be with Bruno Roche, Chief Economist at Mars Inc. at a meeting of the European Economic Summit, of which I was a founding member. He proposed an 'economics of mutuality.' This is based on the value of the individual.

Starting with the value of the individual, the first task is to develop and invest in Human Capital. Then in the way each individual relates to and interacts with others to develop Social Capital with shared identity and values. And then this should be developed within the framework of our Natural Capital, investing in environmental capital. Lastly, this all leads to developing financial capital.

Bruno Roche stated that if we start with developing Financial Capital as the primary goal, then this will always transpire to the cost of human capital, social capital and environmental capital.   Financial Capital is the fruit of investing in human, social and natural capital and is only needed for liquidity in the system, to facilitate exchange. Bruno said, "Focus on developing human, social and natural capital and the shared financial capital will follow. Don't follow money, money will follow you." [39]

Mutuality is an expression of the tern which is used around 100 times in the New Testament, the so-called 'one-another's.' The Greek word used is *'allelon'* which means "one another, each other; mutually, reciprocally." It is the foundation of Christian community and also a foundation for human interaction which promotes mutual benefit.

The Economics of Mutuality asks the question: How do we do business with a new business model approach that delivers superior business performance by mobilising and managing the different forms of capital beyond just money? [40]

Mutually sharing the benefits from business involves all interested parties. The economics of mutuality maintains that growth is not linked to how much one earns, but how much is shared.

Mutuality - giving and receiving - was emphasised by Martin Luther King. "In a real sense all life is interrelated. All men are caught in an inescapable network of mutuality, tied in a single garment of destiny. Whatever affects one directly, affects all indirectly. I can never be what I ought to be until you are what you ought to be, and you can never be what you ought to be until I am what I ought to be . . . This is the interrelated structure of reality." [41]

Let us use our financial capital to set people free, enabling them to enjoy Human, Social and Natural Capital in all they do!   That is economics of mutuality … mutual remuneration … so that each individual involved in the economic process experiences Shalom …   peace, contentment, completeness, wholeness, well-being and harmony!

One business leader showed how he was redeeming profit by identifying the purpose of his business. He expressed this as:

1. Be an economically viable organisation.
2. Value people over money, expressed through giving people the opportunity to live up to their God-given potential.
3. Build up a "good place" in the communities where we work.

His primary purpose for making a profit (which he calls *being economically viable*) is to support the other two purposes of the business. Valuing people over money refers to developing people, so that they grow professionally, socially and spiritually. Building a 'good place' he considers as is another way to express the line in Jesus's prayer, "Your kingdom come, your will be done on earth as it is in heaven."[42]

Chapter 9: Employment

The hiring of labour is a precondition for production of a wide variety and an increased output of goods. Many products could only possibly be manufactured by people, working together, who bring a variety of skills and talents to the teamwork. Many tasks are too large and complicated for one person to accomplish alone. Working in groups requires planning and managing.

The service industry also requires multiple people to carry out the service to many customers.

We, as financial disciples can imitate God in an employer-employee relationship, where this is carried out in fairness, honesty, love, service, and wisdom.

We can imitate God in the sense of wielding authority with the best interests of our co-workers at heart, to get the task done timely and efficiently. Co-workers can imitate God while following the example of Jesus who was fully obedient to the will of His Father.

Both employers and employees can imitate God by demonstrating love to one-another, in a reflection of the inter-dependence of the Trinity. The employee can seek the best interests of the employer in working hard, conscientiously and to the best of his/her ability. The employer can seek the best interests of the employee by giving accurate job descriptions, sufficient training, and honest pay.

"Do nothing from selfish ambition or conceit, but in humility count others more significant than yourselves. Let each of you look not only to his own interests, but also to the interests of others." (Philippians 2:3-5)

By working together to produce goods or deliver services, employers and employees can create wealth for many people.

Paul gave some guidelines for financial disciples at work, to both employers and employees. "Bondservants, obey in everything those who are your earthly masters, not by way of eye-service, as people-pleasers, but with sincerity of heart, fearing the Lord. Whatever you do, work heartily, as for the Lord and not for men, knowing that from the Lord you will receive the inheritance as your reward. You are serving the Lord Christ." (Colossians 3:22-24). As you are serving Christ, you need not fear of an employer treating you wrongly. He will be dealt with by your real employer - God. "For the wrongdoer will be paid back for the wrong he has done, and there is no partiality." (Colossians 3:25)

To the employer, Paul says, "Masters, treat your bondservants justly and fairly, knowing that you also have a Master in heaven." (Colossians 4:1) Masters were not allowed to threaten their servants. "Masters, do the same to them, and stop your threatening, knowing that he who is both their Master and yours is in heaven, and that there is no partiality with him." (Ephesians 6:9) The basic principle is that employers are accountable to God for how they treat employees.

The dark side

Employer-employee relationships are surrounded by temptations to sin.

An employer can misuse his authority and abuse the time and work of the employee; maybe treating him unfairly. Employees could be underpaid.

Wages could even be held back which is, in God's eyes, extremely serious. "Behold, the wages of the labourers who mowed your fields, which you kept back by fraud, are crying out against you, and the cries of the harvesters have reached the ears of the Lord of hosts." (James 5:4)

Employees could be careless in their work. "Whoever is slack in his work is a brother to him who destroys." (Proverbs 18:9) Laziness was a problem in Thessalonica. "For we hear that some among you walk in idleness, not busy at work, but busybodies. Now such persons we command and encourage in the Lord Jesus Christ to do their work quietly and to earn their own living." (2 Thessalonians 3:11,12)

I have hired many people in my career, and one of the most common problems is the lack of truth. I have seen so many people who lie on their CV's to start with! "Truthful lips endure for ever, but a lying tongue lasts only a moment." (Proverbs 12:19)

The Bible explains that in the latter days, which we are surely living in right now, peoples will become enslaved to work. Babylon is used in the Bible to illustrate fallen business and markets. Amongst all the trade people will become objects of buying and selling. "And the merchants of the earth weep and mourn for her, since no one buys their cargo anymore, cargo of gold, silver, jewels, pearls, fine linen, purple cloth, silk, scarlet cloth, all kinds of scented wood, all kinds of articles of ivory, all kinds of articles of costly wood, bronze, iron and marble, cinnamon, spice, incense, myrrh, frankincense, wine, oil, fine flour, wheat, cattle and sheep, horses and chariots, and slaves, that is, human souls." (Revelation 18:11-13)

The merchants engaged in human trafficking and thereby showed they totally disregarded human beings as God's creation (Exodus 21:16). We often think that slavery is a thing of the past. It is certainly not. People all over the world are still being abused, kidnapped, and forced into slave labour.

Redeeming employment

The great management writer Dr. Peter Drucker stated, "If by off-loading employee relations, organisations also lose their capacity to develop people, they will have made a devil's bargain indeed." [43]

"It's not so important to you, as to what your employee can do to make your business profitable as it is what you can do to make it more profitable for your employees. No matter what your business is, your real business is to develop people."[44]

During my time as managing director at a company specialising in human spaceflight services, we were able to employ any highly skilled engineers, scientists, and medical specialists. An aspect of the purpose of our business was not to maximise profits but maximise employment. We knew that people who are happy in their work, skilled at their trade and working for a purpose higher than themselves would make profits.

But more than that, we wanted as many people as possible to come into our 'sphere of influence' as Christian leaders. We looked on all our employees as disciples. People who, through our work and life, could start on a journey of learning who Jesus is and what he could mean to them.

The strap line under our logo stated, "It's all about people." People are worth investing in. In fact, we spent more than our competitors on training that they could give the best service possible to developing space projects. I remember someone asking me, "You spend a lot on training your people. What happens if they leave and you have spent a lot training them?" My reply was, "I prefer to think about what would happen if they stayed and we don't train them!"

Redeeming employment is to follow the simple mission statement of Jesus. "For even the Son of Man came not to be served but to serve, and to give his life as a ransom for many." (Mark 10:45) This is a dual mission. Firstly, to serve people, which means to help them achieve their goals and meet their needs. Secondly, to invest your life to set them free; free to be all they can become, professionally, materially, and spiritually.

Redeemed employment is following the advice of the senior advisors to King Rehoboam when confronted with a request from the people to lighten their financial burden. "And they said to him, "If you will be a servant to this people today and serve them and speak good words to them when you answer them, then they will be your servants forever." (1 Kings 12:7)

The way to build lasting, reciprocal relationships is to serve one another and know how to give good answers.

Chapter 10: Accounting

Accounting is a system for collecting, categorising, and communicating financial information to use in evaluating an organisation's financial health and in making decisions. Financial statements include balance sheets, cash flow information, costs and income statements, as well as management decisions.

Luca Pacioli, Italian mathematician, Franciscan friar, and collaborator with Leonardo da Vinci, is referred to as 'The Father of Accounting and Bookkeeping'. He was the first person to describe the double-entry system of book-keeping. We still teach and use this method today.

His accounting method was a fruit of his theology. [45] He described this in terms of stewards telling the truth to the owners towards whom they have an ethical obligation to give an account. The fundamental equation of double-entry bookkeeping is 'assets - liability = capital.' This is just a representation of a moral truth; once a corporation has discharged its debts, whatever remains belongs to the owner.

Simply stated, everything a company owns represents either an obligation to a creditor or to the owner. [46]

The discipline of accounting reflects our accountability before God. "So then each of us will give an account of himself to God." (Romans 14:12)

"No creature is hidden from him, but all things are naked and exposed to the eyes of him to whom we must give an account." (Hebrews 4:13)

These passages share how we're accountable for our words, our deeds, and even our very selves. Whether or not we make ourselves accountable in this life, we are ultimately accountable to God. One day we'll stand before God himself and give an account. Our accountability to God in this ultimate sense forms the basis for our accountability to one another as human beings.

In the Christian Business Review, Fall 2019, Susan van Weelden and Laureen Mardichian wrote a very helpful article on how accountants can reflect the image of God in their work. [47]

"Being accountable reflects an aspect of the image of God that every human has stamped in our beings, and we are to be accountable to Him as to how we have been faithful to His nature in truthfulness, justice, and love.

The principles of stewardship and accountability are biblical concepts, discussed in the Parables of the Tenants, the Talents, and Shrewd Manager. (Matthew 21:33-46; Matthew 25:14-30; and Luke 16:1-15.) In these parables, resources given are to be managed by servants to grow those resources. The servants are required to give an account of their management of the owner's resources.

God created people as social beings to live in mutually accountable relationships. Mutual accountability is the glue which holds relationships together; "submitting to one another out of reverence for Christ. (Ephesians 5:21)

We are image bearers of God, and our accounting reflects God's image when we demonstrate His characteristics. Three important attributes of God, which are relevant to the roles fulfilled by accountants are justice, righteousness, and honesty. Therefore, information which accountants provide should also be just, righteous, and honest.

We reflect the nature and character of God when we provide an accurate judgement on the financial state of a business. Biblical commands to use 'honest balances, honest weights,' or accurate measures of the success of a business, are part of righteousness. "You shall do no wrong in judgment, in measures of length or weight or quantity. You shall have just balances, just weights, a just ephah, and a just hin: I am the LORD your God, who brought you out of the land of Egypt." (Leviticus 19:35,36)

Justice and righteousness are key characteristics of God. "God is not unjust…." (Hebrews 6:10), "The righteousness of God is revealed through faith for faith" (Romans 1:17)

Fairness or impartiality must be demonstrated by accountants so they do not offer biased financial information to a particular interested party, such as a creditor, or to get a bank loan. " (end quote)

The Bible also describes honesty, or truthfulness, as part of God's character. When God says, "You shall not bear false witness against your neighbour" (Exodus 20:16), He commands us never to lie and to stay away from any kind of deceit. "Love does not delight in evil but rejoices with the truth." (1 Cor. 13:6) "So then, putting away falsehood, let all of us speak truthfully to our neighbours" (Ephesians 4:25). These general requirements for honesty extend, of course, to the accounting profession.

The accounting term of 'representational faithfulness' is just another way of saying 'honesty in all dealings.'

Accountants should give financial statements that enables us to 'love our neighbour as ourselves.' Our neighbour is anyone who has a stake in the organisation, such as shareholders, creditors, employees, managers, government authorities, and the community.

In an ideal world, free from dishonesty, misrepresentation, lying and cheating, we would not need the discipline of accounting as was demonstrated in the building of the Temple in 2 Kings 12:16. "No accounts were kept with the men to whom the money was paid over to be spent on workmen since they were honest in their dealings."

This is virtually repeated in 2 Kings 22:7. Of course, accounts would have been kept if the contractors were less than honest. Alas, accounting is necessary to keep out fraud.

The dark side

Man's capacity for stealing, cheating and lying makes it important to have a system that reduces this temptation. (Malachi 7:5,6) "Put no trust in a neighbour, have no confidence in a friend."   Unfortunately, human nature requires effective internal control systems. A healthy scepticism is needed.

Companies are complex and diverse enough to enable managers and accountants to 'cook the books.'

The dark side of accounting is seen when assets are overstated or liabilities are understated to make a business appear financially stronger than it really is.

False accounting occurs when an employee alters or

destroys any record or presents accounts which do not truly reflect the financial activities of that company. This could happen for a number of reasons; to get bank loans; reporting unrealistic profits; hiding losses; or covering up theft.

Companies are confronted with falsifying accounts when an employee makes inflated expense claims, or when a manager tries to cover up trading losses or fraudulent activity.

A basic ethic for accurate accounting must be honesty. The basis for the efficiency of an honest information system lies in the character of God. He loves truth because he is truth, as Jesus said in John 14:6. God hates dishonesty.

There is potential for abuse in accounting due to the accrual process, which contains potential for managers to manipulate profits by changing the period when income and costs are recorded.

Redeeming accounting

Accounting rules and regulations exist to make sure that financial statements are accurate so that users can make decisions based on a truthful financial state of the organisation. To be useful, the information presented must be produced in time and accurately reflect the financial circumstances. When the accounting process is not honest, this can induce fraud, stealing and harm the organisation's reputation.

Formalising accounting laws, rules and regulations is unfortunately, not sufficient to prevent dishonesty. Such character traits as received through the Spirit of God are needed. People cannot be forced to be honest, no matter how many rules are in force, so we need to find honest people to do the work! Even corrupt people want non-corrupt people handling their money!

A supreme example of redeemed accounting which brings glory to God and reflects His nature, can be found in Daniel. In Babylon, the emperor Darius appointed regional leaders, called satraps. He also appointed three higher officials to whom the satraps should be accountable for his finances. One of these was Daniel.

"Then this Daniel became distinguished above all the other high officials and satraps because an excellent spirit was in him. And the king planned to set him over the whole kingdom. Then the high officials and the satraps sought to find a ground for complaint against Daniel with regard to the kingdom, but they could find no ground for complaint or any fault, because he was faithful, and no error or fault was found in him." (Daniel 6:3,4)

The Spirit of God gave Daniel managing and financial skills together with complete incorruptibility and honesty. The satraps and the other officials were jealous of Daniel, doing their best to find fault in him, but couldn't. They then sought to attack Daniel on religious grounds. God rem gained faithful to Daniel despite all the persecution.

Paul warned Timothy, "Indeed, all who desire to live a godly life in Christ Jesus will be persecuted, while evil people and impostors will go on from bad to worse, deceiving and being deceived." (2 Timothy3:12,13.

Accounting is making the invisible, visible. This is a very important Biblical principle for a healthy cooperation both with The Lord and with our co-workers.. "God is light, and in him is no darkness at all. If we say we have fellowship with him while we walk in darkness, we lie and do not practice the truth. But if we walk in the light, as he is in the light, we have fellowship with one another, and the blood of Jesus his Son cleanses us from all sin." (1 John 1:6,7)

A penetrating question to help in decision-making is,

"Can it come into the light? Can it be widely known? Or is there something which you want hidden?"

Transparency is an essential quality in following Jesus and working with others in business.

Chapter 11: Taxation

Jesus gave a brilliant answer to some religious leaders who tried to trap him with a question for which any answer he might give could create serious trouble for him from one authority or another. "Show me a denarius. Whose likeness and inscription does it have?" They said, "Caesar's." 25 He said to them, "Then render to Caesar the things that are Caesar's, and to God the things that are God's." (Luke 20:24-25)

They asked, "Is it lawful for us to pay taxes to Caesar or not?" (Luke 20:22) In other words, "Should we pay taxes to this Gentile government, or should we withhold them?"

Jesus, knowing their hypocrisy, said to them, "Why put me to the test? Bring me a denarius and let me look at it." And they brought one. And he said to them, "Whose likeness and inscription is this?" They said to him, "Caesar's." Jesus said to them, "Render therefore to Caesar the things that are Caesar's, and to God the things that are God's." And they marvelled at him.

John Piper in his article, "Render to Caesar the Things

That Are Caesar's" explains this statement in an enlightening way.[48] "What is God's? Everything. So the point seems to be that when you realise that all of life, including all of Caesar's rights and power and possessions, belong to God, then you will be in a proper frame of mind to render to Caesar what is due to Caesar. When you know that all is God's, then anything you render to Caesar will be done for God's sake. Any authority you ascribe to Caesar you will ascribe to him for the sake of God's greater authority. Any obedience you render to Caesar you will render for the sake of the obedience you owe first to God. Any claim Caesar makes on you, you test by the infinitely higher claim God has on you."

Things belong to Caesar only because God alone determined and permitted his limited claims to accomplish His own divine plan.

Jesus and Peter call Christians to live both as citizens and foreigners. *"Live as people who are free, not using your freedom as a cover-up for evil, but living as servants of God"* (1 Peter 2:16, ESV). We serve God, not a government or any institution. We belong to God, who owns the entire universe, and are all *"fellow heirs with Christ"* (Romans 8:17, ESV). We all share God's inheritance; God has made us and bought us for Himself.

Because we are free from Caesar and this earthly realm, God commissions us to join society to be *"faithful in that which is another's"* (Luke 16:12, ESV). While on earth, we will live according to the ideas of our current society. We exist with this dissonance within two kingdoms.

This is stewardship in action. I like to pay the tax that belongs to the government – first of all because I love God and want to respect His will. And because paying taxes is an act of obedience, it means I have to be completely honest in my tax returns. I have to admit that I have not been very faithful to this in the past. There is a great temptation to conceal some income. However, honesty and truth are prerequisites for God's blessing.

The second reason I am thankful to pay taxes is that it means I am earning something. This is a sign of God's provision.

As a financial disciple, you will thank God for the income He has provided, even though you may think it isn't enough. Remember, God makes no mistakes. Thank God for the way in which you can help facilitate the work of the government to provide necessary services through your taxes. God provides so that you can also meet the needs of others; this includes all your fellow citizens. Turn your tax return into an offer of thanks to God!

All that this world provides has been entrusted to us by God in stewardship. All that the next world offers has been purchased for us by Another, by Jesus himself, through His sacrificial death. It becomes our own through the obedience of faith. As we demonstrate trustworthiness with the material things of this world, God entrusts to us the true treasures – not because we deserve them but because God has graced them to us in and through Jesus. To base our lives on this truth is to demonstrate real wisdom.

The dark side

When the people asked for a king, God warned them about excessive taxation. That story is told in I Samuel 8, and in verses 11-18, Samuel told them that the king would many good things for himself and make them his servants. God gave them a king.

After Solomon died, his son Rehoboam took his place. Solomon may have been the wisest man who ever lived, but his extensive building projects placed a heavy, almost unbearable burden on the shoulders of the people.

People came to Rehoboam to ask if their tax burden could be eased. "Your father made our yoke heavy. Now therefore lighten the hard service of your father and his heavy yoke on us, and we will serve you." (1 Kings 12:4)

Rehoboam was not asked to completely remove the burden, just lighten it a bit so that they could handle it. It was not an unreasonable request.

The King took counsel from the older, wiser men who had served his father. They replied, "And they said to him, "If you will be a servant to this people today and serve them, and speak good words to them when you answer them, then they will be your servants forever." (1 Kings 12:6)

However, he choose the counsel of the younger men who had grown up with him. Their advice was to make the burden heavier.   The King said to the people, "My father made your yoke heavy, but I will add to your yoke. My father disciplined you with whips, but I will discipline you with scorpions (special whips)." (I Kings 12:14)

Rehoboam answered the people "roughly," that is, with harshness in his voice. He was the last king to rule a united kingdom. It was soon to be split.

We should always be careful what we ask for; we might just get it.

Unfair taxes leads to 'harshness,' causing individual and corporate distress and to loss of unity.

Harsh taxation can easily lead to corruption, lying, stealing and fraud. However, disagreeing with the government is not a legitimate reason to not pay taxes.

Inability to pay taxes due is symptomatic of poor financial planning.

Taxes should never be a source of cash flow problems. When taxes due are not planned for, accrued or reserved, a tax demand from the government can cause us financial hardship. Failure to plan and reserve for taxes is one of the most common causes for bankruptcy.

Redeeming taxation

Zaccheus gives us a good example of redeeming taxation. When he invites Jesus into his life, something changes. Zaccheus declares, "Look, half of my possessions, Lord, I will give to the poor; and if I have defrauded anyone of anything, I will pay back four times as much" (Luke 19:8).

He promised to use his money to help the poor and to conduct his business dealings honestly and make restitution for any dishonest dealings of the past. Zaccheus had used his occupation as a tax collector to enrich the Roman occupiers and himself through extortion and had dedicated himself to serve money. After meeting Jesus he started using his resources to serve his neighbours, and by extension to serve God.

Some tax collectors approached the disciples asking of their Master paid taxes. In His answer to Peter, Jesus indicated that the sons of the Kingdom should be free from the duty to pay taxes., as are the sons of earthly rulers. However, not toggle offence, which could cause reprisals, Jesus asked `Peter to go fishing, cast a hook and look in the mouth of the first fish you catch. Peter found a shekel with which he could pay the tax.

Looking at some previous scenes involving fish, we see that twice, in Matt 14 and 15, Jesus exerted God's sovereignty over fish, multiplying small fish to feed crowds. Rome claimed that the emperor owns the sea and its creatures. and taxed the fishing industry. However, the sea and its creatures belong to God, and are subject to God's sovereignty. God supplied a fish with the coin in its mouth.

Disciples are to pay their taxes. This may seem to be submissive and complacent to the word's rulers, but for disciples, it testifies to God's sovereignty and His provision of all we need to follow His ways.

The Bible commands us to pay taxes to whom they are due. "Pay to all what is owed to them: taxes to whom taxes are owed, revenue to whom revenue is owed, respect to whom respect is owed, honour to whom honour is owed." (Romans 13:7) Whenever He gives us a command, he will always grant us the resources we need to carry out that command! He always pays for what he orders!

Chapter 12: Generosity

Generosity is one of the most important characteristics of the financial disciple in the workplace. It is said that "you are never more like Jesus than when you are giving." We imitate the essential nature of God by giving. Good has designed us to share and be generous.

In order imitate God, we can contribute to develop a culture of generosity in the business or the area in which we work. Generosity is about caring for the interests of others. "Do nothing from selfish ambition or conceit, but in humility count others more significant than yourselves. Let each of you look not only to his own interests, but also to the interests of others." (Philippians 2:3,4)

What does it mean to be a generous colleague? Generous colleagues share information readily, give credit where due, and give their time to help and share their expertise

Generous colleagues create a comfortable, friendly environment and develop community. Willingness to share helps form strong relationships and that will stimulate productivity. Generous colleagues help others succeed without expecting anything in return.

We can practice generosity by being attentive and being there for them to help them solve their problems. "Bear one another's burdens, and so fulfil the law of Christ." (Galatians 6:2)

We can practice generosity through active listening. An inability to listen to others leads to misunderstanding and potential conflict. Ask what their needs are and look for ways to help them. "Know this, my beloved brothers: let every person be quick to hear, slow to speak, slow to anger." (James 1:19)

We can practice generosity by offering opportunities to help them forward, to give them space to grow, to excel. We can be generous in giving promotions, raises, bonuses, referrals, and recognition where and when they're due.
"Do not withhold good from those to whom it is due, when it is in your power to do it." (Proverbs 3:27)

We can practice generosity by encouraging people to do their best and help them practically and emotionally when things don't turn out well. Thanking your co-workers for their contribution is always encouraging. "Therefore encourage one another and build one another up, just as you are doing." (1 Thessalonians 5:11)

The workplace with its many diverse people, relationships and challenges is an ideal arena for developing generosity.

The dark side

The dark side of generosity is 'withholding.' "One gives freely yet grows all the richer; another withholds what he should give, and only suffers want." (Proverbs 11:24)

We are designed to be generous givers. Withholding means to refuse to give; to suppress or hold back.

There are several enemies to generosity which form the dark side.

- Disinterest. The state of just not caring. Teddy Roosevelt shared some great wisdom. "No one cares how much you know, until they know how much you care."
- Fear. Fear of not having enough money. "Keep your life free from love of money, and be content with what you have, for he has said, "I will never leave you nor forsake you." (Hebrews 13:5)
- Greed. The ugly head of greed and discontentment does more than keep us from giving: It keeps us from enjoying what we have. Jesus said to a business guy, "Watch out! Be on your guard against all kinds of greed; life does not consist in an abundance of possessions." (Luke 12:15)
- Selfishness. People tend to focus on the loss of buying power as a result of giving. Jesus teaches us to replace selfishness with generosity by demonstrating hospitality to thousands of people where the disciples are concerned about budget availability. (See Mark 6:31-44)
- Cynicism. We need to be willing to help even if sometimes people will take advantage of us. Only one of the lepers Jesus healed came back to thank Him. (See Luke 17:11-19)
- Distance. Instead of ignoring the needs around you, serve the needy in your company and get

around people who are suffering. (See Matthew 25:34-40)

- Expecting a return: Generosity does not expect anything in return. People will know when you have a double agenda. "But love your enemies, and do good, and lend, expecting nothing in return, and your reward will be great, and you will be sons of the Most High, for he is kind to the ungrateful and the evil." (Luke 6:35)

God told Abraham to release the most precious thing he had to Him, his son, Isaac. On hiking up the mountain together, Abraham was ready to sacrifice his son, when they encountered an angel, sent from God. "He said, "Do not lay your hand on the boy or do anything to him, for now I know that you fear God, seeing you have not withheld your son, your only son, from me." (Genesis 22:12)

Are you withholding anything from God?

When we realise that we belong to God together with our career, our talents, skills and education, our relationships, our ambitions, then withholding these things from the Lord, means that we cannot use them and we miss the blessing!

"Do not withhold good from those to whom it is due, when it is in your power to do it." (Proverbs 3:27)

Redeeming generosity

The National Christian Foundation gave a good description of a generous business. "The generous business is not just about the bottom-line or making the owners wealthier, it's about taking care of employees and customers while changing their environment.

It is important for people to feel like they a part of something bigger than themselves. People get enthusiastic when they know that the time and talents that they are using during the business day will produce benefits that will be used to help others in my community and throughout the world. Most people view their job as a way to earn money, pay the bills and support their family. Life is much more fulfilling when the purpose at work is not just to draw wages. A generous company is committed to challenging its owners, staff, and families to lead transformative change through the joy of giving.

While a generosity programme often starts with a generous owner, the vision for generous giving goes well beyond the owner and culminates with staff members and their families passionately giving from their resources as they seek to transform their environment. A generous company creates a culture of stewardship where staff members are actively engaged in the giving culture." [49]

Mark Mitchell is CEO of the largest independent car distributors in the north of England. He and his wife have been working actively to develop a generous company.

"We've created a staff of people we really enjoy, employees with character and passion, who work together for a bigger and more meaningful purpose. And, if entire families get involved, the company becomes a more important and valuable part of each of their lives."

He lists some of the benefits:

- By participating in the community and with charities, their staff has developed stronger leadership, teamwork, and networking skills as they have helped address various social and economic situations together.
- People think about spending differently as they see how spending impacts their ability to give to causes they support. Every dollar really does impact a program.

-      As their employees' passion for giving grows, they have been willing to help the business grow, so they can have an even greater impact.
-      Their customers and business partners have become stronger supporters as they learn about the company's purpose and integrity in giving. Customers are given 'days out' with their family, driving the latest cars.

Giving a part of the income, or assets of a company reflects acknowledgement of the source of wealth in the business. "You shall remember the LORD your God, for it is he who gives you power to get wealth, that he may confirm his covenant that he swore to your fathers, as it is this day." (Deuteronomy 8:18)

When preparing for the building of the Temple, David acknowledged that people were only giving back what God had given them in the first place. "But who am I, and what is my people, that we should be able thus to offer willingly? For all things come from you, and of your own have we given you." (1 Chronicles 29:14)

Some Questions To Consider

1. Chapter 1 describes eight ways in which finance facilitates serving God, stewarding creation and serving our 'neighbours' at work.

   a. Which resonates the most with you?

   b. How have you experienced the 'dark side' of financial transactions?

2. The next chapters described 11 aspects of financial management, using the framework of creation, fall and redemption.
   Each of the 11 aspects of financial activities at work begins with our call to glorify God in all we do.

   How can you imitate God in carrying out the various aspects of finances in your workplace?

4. In each of the 11 aspects of financial functions, Peter describes how sin can cause adverse, unwanted effects.

   How can you recognise when the dark side of financial actions is becoming visible?

   How have you experienced these adverse effects in the past?

5.   Peter describes how negative effects of these 11 functions can be redeemed.

How can activities which go against God's principles be redeemed?

With which of the 11 functions of finance are you struggling with right now?

How can you partner with the Lord to redeem this and restore God's best practice?

Part 3. Finance Decisions - by the Book

The Bible gives us a complete source of help in handling financial matters at work. "All Scripture is breathed out by God and profitable for teaching, for reproof, for correction, and for training in righteousness, that the man/woman of God may be complete, equipped for every good work." (2 Timothy 3:16)

Unfortunately, Biblical teaching on handling money is very rare in our churches. However, the Bible has so much to say about managing money - God's way, not only your own private finances but also the company's finances.

We can imitate the Lord by following His instructions on many various topics and dilemma's relating to finances at work.

Here are 14 decision areas as examples of how the Bible help us to manage finances - God's way.

At the end of this Part 3, there are a few questions for you to consider.

Chapter 1: Paying Wages

A good principle for a disciple, who strives to achieve God's objectives, is that he treats employees and colleagues, with whom he has been entrusted, as his family. God is primarily interested in relationships, and a guiding question in decisions over salary is, "how would I treat her if she was my daughter?" The salary policy of the employer is defined by those two qualities, described by Micah. Act justly and love kindness. "He has told you, O man, what is good; and what does the LORD require of you but to do justice, and to love kindness, and to walk humbly with your God? (Micah 6:8)

As Christians, we are accountable to the Lord for paying our employees a fair wage, on time. The question of what constitutes a fair wage is a tough one. Business needs and personal needs often conflict. Timothy argues that a Christian employer will want to help their employees to provide for their families. (1 Timothy 5:8) Rewarding employees for excellent work, is a principle used by Luke's account of Jesus rewarding servants who used the money entrusted to them well. (Luke 19)

James gives stern warnings about not paying wages on time. "Behold, the wages of the labourers who mowed your fields, which you kept back by fraud, are crying out against you, and the cries of the harvesters have reached the ears of the Lord of hosts." (James 5:4)

Jesus used an illustration of a master returning and holding his manager accountable for the way he is looking after the master's business. He says, ""Who then is the faithful and wise servant, whom his master has set over his household, to give them their food at the proper time? Blessed is that servant whom his master will find so doing when he comes. Truly, I say to you, he will set him over all his possessions." (Matthew 24:45-47)

In our business of delivering specialised services to the European Space Agency, our main competitive advantage was our people. The Lord brought many capable people to our business to conduct the services required in space science, safety, and engineering. Our customers depended on support from well trained and satisfied people. In fact, our customers at the Agency knew we paid our employees well, because contract proposals needed to be transparent and show costs, even what salaries we paid. We were never the cheapest, but our customers knew our people were good at their jobs! During the start-up of our company, we sometimes had to go without salaries ourselves in order to pay our employees!

How are you paying your employees? According to God's plan for them? Justly, fairly, and out of love for their wellbeing?

Here are some Biblical principles to consider when working through remuneration issues.

God takes the side of personnel who are being exploited and makes a special case for widows and orphans. "So I will come to put you on trial. I will be quick to testify against sorcerers, adulterers, and perjurers, against those who defraud labourers of their wages, who oppress the widows and the fatherless, and deprive the foreigners among you of justice, but do not fear me,' says the Lord Almighty." (Malachi 3:5)

Not only do we want to avoid God putting us on trial for unfair treatment of employees' wages, but we should also know that conviction carries a sentence! God will punish unfair payment of personnel. "Look! The wages you failed to pay the workers who mowed your fields are crying out against you. The cries of the harvesters have reached the ears of the Lord Almighty." (James 5:4) (see also Deut. 24:15,16)

A basic principle is that we should help employees to provide for their families, as the family is God's basic unit for a well-functioning society. "Anyone who does not provide for their relatives, and especially for their own household, has denied the faith and is worse than an unbeliever" (1 Tim 5:8)

Good work should be rewarded. Jesus told two parables about a master rewarding his servants for excellent work, "The first one came and said, 'Sir, your mina has earned ten more.' 'Well done, my good servant!' his master replied. 'Because you have been trustworthy in a very small matter, take charge of ten cities.'" (Luke 19:16,17) Some system of rewarding achievement is fair and just and is a strong motivating factor for employees.

Chapter 2: Being Accountable

Businesspeople are often strong personalities who want to go it alone. Our culture of individuality is not conducive to accountability. The verse from Frank Sinatra rings loud and clear, "I did it my way!" However, this is not the way of the Christian seeking to imitate the Lord in business. We have been called to be part of a Body of believers and we are accountable, not only to the Master, but also to one another.

At the core of financial discipleship is 'accountability', the need to be accountable/responsible to God and to fellow man. Our accountability to God is a model for the need for accountability in our own affairs. The standard is very high – God's holiness. "Walk before me, faithfully, and be blameless," says God. (Genesis 17:1,2)

The Lord will hold us fully accountable for our actions.

Accountability to our superiors, equals and those under us, in a 360-degree accountability, helps us in living out an authentic faith in the marketplace, and helps to protect us from taking a wrong path. "Iron sharpens iron, and one man sharpens another." (Proverbs 27:17)

The Bible says that being accountable is essential in applying Jesus' teachings in our business. The Proverbs tell us that heading advice provides protection and raises the effectiveness of the business in honouring God through all our decisions.

I have been in business for more than 40 years, and all that time, I have been a member of groups of Christian businesspeople. In these groups we discuss business dilemma's and discover together what counsel and guidance the Bible gives. We then pray over our difficulties and our challenges, asking the Lord to reveal His wisdom to us. I have found that there has never been a problem in business which I have faced, which someone else in the group has not already been through! Advice from fellow Christians in business has helped to prevent me making wrong choices! Getting help to work through my dilemma's has saved me a lot of money, by preventing making wrong choices! It is a rewarding investment in time and money to belong to such Christian business accountability groups! Such accountability provides direction, security and encouragement.

At the last company of which I was CEO, we instigated a "Council of Advisors" to operate as an accountability group for our business. They were a kind of 'spiritual board of directors.' They were not given executive powers, but we took their advice extremely seriously. We met quarterly for four to six hours and shared our business results, problems and dilemmas with them, receiving very valuable advice. There were four members this Council of Advisors - an accountant, a business owner of a similar business to ours, a lawyer, and a consultant who took notes and gave us a detailed report of our meetings. The first three advisors donated their time to help us develop a business which would be useful for the purposes of the Kingdom. We paid the consultant for his time, as he had to spend time preparing the agenda, writing reports and helping us follow up on commitments. This was a wonderful investment which not only helped us to avoid some otherwise costly mistakes but helped us to solve some troubling issues and make some effective plans for future growth.

Accountability requires openness, and the willingness to be vulnerable. I have found, in business, that vulnerability is a surprising way of connecting to others. In business, we tend to keep our cards very close to our chests, often very suspicious of what people might do with our information. Of course, choosing your accountability partners must be done very carefully. Trustworthy people are scarce. "Many will say they are loyal friends, but who can find one who is truly reliable?" (Proverbs 20:6 NLT) I have made this a matter of prayer, that the Lord will bring me to the right people.

Would Jesus be pleased with your choices in accounting, operations, sales, and human resource management? He will hold you accountable to make your choices – Biblically. Do you have friends in business who can give you godly counsel and help you work through your problems? God often works though other believers to communicate His will to us!

Being accountable is an essential exercise in applying the teachings of Jesus in our business practice. It provides protection, produces good advice and raises the effectiveness of the business in honouring God through all decisions and in all relationships.

Accountability is the most powerful tool to develop self-control; the last aspect mentioned in the fruit of the Spirit, but I think the one which facilitates the rest. As we are encouraged to let go of our independent spirit, this leaves more room for the Holy Spirit to produce His fruit in us.

Our need to be accountable is an acknowledgement of our need for an independent review of our actions and decisions. We need this review to grow and to mature in Christ. "Submit to one another out of reverence for Christ.." (Ephesians 5:21) Accountability and the growth in character it stimulates, will better equip us to live authentic Christian lives in the secular marketplace.

Chapter 3: Paying Invoices

It is said that 'your best client is the one who pays on time!' That is certainly true and for Christians in business, paying on time is a good testimony. Conversely, if our suppliers know that we are Christians and we are not paying on time, then it can destroy our testimony. Meeting our financial obligations, fully and on time, is a basic requirement to love our neighbour, as Paul told Roman believers. Paying what is due, is a demonstration of love. "Pay to all what is owed to them: taxes to whom taxes are owed, revenue to whom revenue is owed, respect to whom respect is owed, honour to whom honour is owed." (Romans 13:7,8)

If I make an agreement to pay personnel or a supplier within a particular timeframe and I fail to do so, then I have broken a promise and I put my reputation at risk. Christ lives in us does not want to be involved in the breaking of promises. He always keeps his word! "The wicked borrows but does not pay back, but the righteous is generous and gives." (Psalm 37:21)

It should be a priority to pay everyone in time, not only for my own reputation but also to honour God! Indeed, the Psalm says that not paying back what we owe is sinful. Jesus said that if we have a conflict, we should settle this quickly with our adversary, otherwise our offers to the Lord will be ignored!

Paying on time can improve my credit rating and reputation with suppliers and help to secure timely deliveries with good terms and long-lasting contracts.

The development of healthy, long-lasting relationships is indispensable for the business. We shouldn't see relationships with creditors suffer for allowing a bill, salary, or debt remain unpaid. My 'credit-ability' is an important aspect of my witness as a Christian in the marketplace.

As our controlling Partner in business, the Lord's role is to supply what the business needs. "And God is able to bless you abundantly, so that in all things at all times, having all that you need, you will abound in every good work." (2 Corinthians 9:8). This will be enough to pay all our obligations regarding salaries, suppliers, taxes, and owners' dividends in a timely way.

When I was CEO of a chemical company, most of our products were based on oil derivatives. Some time ago, there was an oil crisis and supplies were short. Some raw materials were even being rationed. I remember receiving a visit from one of our suppliers, a large German chemical business. The representative asked how much of a particular product we needed for our production. I told him what we would need for the coming months. 'OK,' he said, 'you have it.' I was surprised at his reaction because we were not a large user of his products. I asked why we were receiving preferential treatment. He replied, "because you always pay your invoices before the due date!"

How is your reputation with your suppliers? Does this glorify God?

Not meeting all of our obligations fully and timely, can cause us to slip into debt. You can slip very easily into debt, spiritually and morally speaking, occurs when four aspects of your business are not being conducted in a godly way. I am in debt when I do not keep promises I have made. If I say I will pay a bill at such and such a date, and I fail to do this, then I am involving God in a deceitful situation. I find this extremely serious and a reason for me to always take extra good care of my cash flow. I never want to get inti a situation that I involve God in breaking a promise. The Bible is clear that "God is not man, that he should lie, or a son of man, that he should change his mind. Has he said, and will he not do it? Or has he spoken, and will he not fulfil it?"

This has enormous consequences for my cash flow. I always spent a lot of time planning the flow of cash in the business, to make sure I would always have enough cash to meet current payables. This not always easy. It could mean negotiating with suppliers to extend their credit period and negotiating with customers to shorten the credit we give to them. Taking trouble to communicate with suppliers and customers can yield good results.

It also means to have an efficient collection policy, ensuring that customers are paying on time. More about this in a later chapter.

It becomes really tough when customers are not paying on time. When I have been consulting others, I have often heard, "Peter, my business is having serious cash flow problems. I owe a variety of suppliers about €80,000, and all of it is over 90 days due. I also have seven employees who expect to be paid on Friday. Who do I pay first?" I believe that our employees are our immediate 'neighbours' and serve their pay first - above paying ourselves. I have once had to go without pay for 3 months in order to meet the payroll. This is a very stressful situation. It may mean having to cut staff and expenses to help us meet our promises to suppliers who also constitute, 'our neighbours,' spiritually.

At a conference I attended some years ago, the then CEO of a large chemical company, John Harvey-Jones made a statement which has been a guiding light for me in money management. He said, "Turnover is vanity, profit is sanity, but cash is reality." Many businesspeople measure success by sales growth, especially salesmen. However, if the sales are not profitable, you are filling yourself. Furthermore, if the customers are not laying, then your business could be in trouble. The best measure of business success, financial speaking is cash - money in the bank. A wise old mentor said to me, a sale is not a sale until the cash is in the back!"

I was at a business training seminar early in my career. I remember the presenter saying, ". Developing cash flow on your business is easy. Delay paying your bills as long as you can and pressure your customers for payment as soon as you can." This made my toes curl up in my shoes. What a way to do business? I resolved never to follow that advice. "Do not withhold good from those who deserve it when it's in your power to help them. If you can help your neighbour now, don't say, "Come back tomorrow, and then I'll help you." Don't plot harm against your neighbour, for those who live nearby trust you. Don't pick a fight without reason when no one has done you harm. Don't envy violent people or copy their ways. Such wicked people are detestable to the LORD, but he offers his friendship to the godly." (Proverbs 3:27-32)

Let this be our business-style!

Chapter 4: Extending Credit

How do you deal with lending and credit control in a way that glorifies God?

God promised His people that they would be blessed if they obeyed His commandments. One of those blessings had to do with lending, which is extending credit. Moses indicated that the Lord would bless all the work of your hand; and be able to lend to others. "The LORD will open to you his good treasury, the heavens, to give the rain to your land in its season and to bless all the work of your hands. And you shall lend to many nations, but you shall not borrow." (Deuteronomy 28:12)

Just because lending is part of 'the blessing' doesn't mean we can simply forge ahead without considering how to extend credit in a way that is both honouring to God and consistent with Biblical principles.

Doing business by biblical principles requires that we manage our credit in such a way that we keep bad debts at a minimum. Most companies sue others or turn them over to collection without giving it a second thought. For them, it is simply a part of doing business. We are not to operate like that.

We are to conduct business by a higher standard. Remember, our purpose in business is to glorify God and to sincerely care about customers even if we don't know them personally.

It is imperative that you establish a well-conceived policy for extending credit. Manage your receivables to keep bad debts at a minimum. If you have a customer with an outstanding balance extending beyond 30 or 60 days, communicate, communicate, communicate! They may be using your credit to fund other needs in their company. Become a student of the customers who owe you money. What are vendors or others in the marketplace saying that might indicate your delinquent payers are in trouble?

If customers are unable or unwilling to pay, talk with them to discuss the matter. Then listen. Although you may be frustrated or even angry, remember that your purposes in business include glorifying God and influencing people for Christ. Many businesses routinely sue those who are delinquent without making an effort to preserve the relationship. However, we are not to conduct business like that; we are to genuinely care for others, even if we ultimately turn the debt over to a collection agency.

Many businesses fail because of poor credit policies. Business leaders must be wise in their approach to lending. Business-to-business credit is usually used as a means of managing cash flow. Customers who place orders, expecting credit beyond the permitted payment period, are asking you to be their banker. Be careful not to extend further credit just to make a sale. Make sure you do a credit check on your existing customers on an annual basis as well as on all new customers.

Since you are committed to pay your creditors, whether or not your customers pay you, think carefully about how much credit you extend and to whom. Let these principles be your guide:

- Limit your lending to those who are faithful in repaying. You could consider starting by limiting their credit to see if they are faithful in repaying on time. "One who is faithful in a very little is also faithful in much, and one who is dishonest in a very little is also dishonest in much." (Luke 16:10)

- Evaluate their capacity for credit. "Suppose one of you wants to build a tower. Won't you first sit down and estimate the cost to see if you have enough money to complete it? For if you lay the foundation and are not able to finish it, everyone who sees it will ridicule you, saying, "This person began to build and wasn't able to finish." (Luke 14:28-30)

- Ask yourself, could I be damaged by extending this credit? Would I be willing to write it off if needed? "And if you lend to those from whom you expect repayment, what credit is that to you? Even sinners lend to sinners, expecting to be repaid in full. But love your enemies, do good and lend to them without expecting to get anything back" (Luke 6:34)

Our purpose in business is to glorify God and sincerely care about customers. Jesus indicates that we should 'not turn away' from those you do business with. This extends also to those who have difficulty in paying what is owed. "Give to the one who begs from you, and do not refuse the one who would borrow from you." (Matthew 5:42) Are you financially healthy enough to be able to write off a debt to help those who need it? Again, this is another strong case to develop a strong, positive cashflow, so that you can bless another, when called to do so.

When you work for a public company, you have the legal fiduciary responsibility to act for the benefit of the shareholders. You may not have as much freedom to forgive debts. However, you can still model the love of Christ by your respectful and reasonable communication with those who are past due. In a one-on-one contact in which you show respect for the person, attempt to work out a payment plan. If this fails, encourage the person to meet with a debt or business counsellor.

In our chemical business, we made regular credit checks on customers. This saved us from losing money due to a customer going bankrupt. We also realised that we had a responsibility to those who could not pay. Having made a policy to be debt free and maintain a good cash flow, we were in a position to extend more credit to customers who had genuine payment problems. In one case, we even wrote off a large debt, so that a customer could continue dealing with us, and we could continue to deliver our products. Future profits from this business more than made up for this sacrifice. We did analyse the need of the customer very carefully. If the customer would not pay, and gave no opening of his situation, then we would not think of forgiving the debt. However, if a customer was in genuine need, maintained an open communication with us, then we looked for ways to demonstrate grace.

Chapter 5: Collecting Debts

Decisions about collecting debts are important due to the influence they have on maintaining durable business relationships. Because our business belongs to God, maintaining a good reputation, both for myself and the God we serve, is extremely important.

Management of accounts receivable must be governed by a balance between making sure payments are received within the agreed timeframe, and active cooperation to help solve payment problems.

Jesus was described by John as being 'full of grace and truth.' (John 1:17) We want to deal with our debtors based on truth by delivering good products, keeping our promises, and proactively ensuring payments are received. We also want, as God's representatives, to demonstrate grace to our debtors whenever they have difficulty meeting their obligations to us.

Managing receivables in business is finding this balance

between grace and truth. If a customer genuinely cannot pay, and we would bring him into more trouble by insisting on payment, can we apply grace and help the customer to solve his problem? This may cost us, but the proverb says that a good reputation is better than money! "A good name is to be chosen rather than great riches, and favour is better than silver or gold." (Proverbs 22:1)

If a customer will not pay, and expressly uses us, we should apply truth and do all we can to make him pay– even to a last resort of legal means. The debtor must then be held accountable.

Not paying bills on time is a sure symptom of underlying problems. Are there opportunities to help your customers and show God's grace?

Our company made cleaning and sanitising products for the food industry. One of our independent agents, specialised in the meat processing industry, was an excellent salesman, but (as is often the case) a terrible administrator. He could not pay his invoices on time. This frustrated our credit controller so much that he was threatening legal action which made our agent angry. I decided to step in and visit the agent at his home office. I immediately saw the problem. He did not have a filing system but a 'piling' system. Some invoices were lost, correspondence unopened. We solved the problem by buying his business, taking over his debt, and employing him as a salesman. This gave him a well-paid job, servicing his customers and we managed the invoices. He was very happy and so were we! Applying grace was profitable for both parties.

When customers do not pay our bills, we can often be faced with having to resort to legal means. However, I believe that the principles set out for confronting people as set out in the Bible apply to both believers and non-believers.

How far should we pursue an obligation, assuming that the total decision is ours? If a Christian is under the authority of others who make these decisions, then it is a matter of obeying our authority.

Should a Christian use a collection agency to pursue a non-paying customer? That decision is not an easy one, but every Christian must be aware that God judges attitudes more than actions. The collection agency is representing my company, and I cannot absolve myself by allowing others to violate biblical principles on my behalf.

Last, is the question of lawsuits. Should we pursue recovery of a debt all the way to the courtroom? Fist of all, "To have lawsuits at all with one another is already a defeat for you." (1 Corinthians 6:7) Why is this a defeat for us? Originally, Paul referred to lawsuits with other believers, but I believe this also applies to a breakdown of relationships in general. The Lord's primary wish is to maintain good relationships and restore them quickly when broken. The goal for a Christian must always be reconciliation.

I do have a legal right to take someone to court, but, as Paul would tell us, "All things are lawful for me," but not all things are helpful." (1 Corinthians 6:12a) If I do find myself taking someone to court, then the relationship becomes hostile. We are called to 'love our neighbour as ourselves.' The question we should then ask, 'how would I like my opponent to that me?' The answer gives us a different take on our situation.

This question, in regard to Christians, seems clear from I Corinthians 6:1. "When one of you has a dispute with another believer, how dare you file a lawsuit and ask a secular court to decide the matter instead of taking it to other believers. (NLT) What about non-Christians who owe us? Clearly, if a

Christian is to follow God's **best** in this area of collection, it will require an absolute commitment to our purpose - to glorify God! Remember, it's not just about our reputation, but about God's name!

We should strive to follow the Biblical principle as laid down by Jesus in His sermon. "But I say, do not resist an evil person! If someone slaps you on the right cheek, offer the other cheek also. If you are sued in court and your shirt is taken from you, give your coat, too." (Matthew 5:39,40) If we want to apply grace in this way, we need a very healthy and robust cash flow management to make sure we have the financial capacity to show grace and mercy.

I have never had to take a person to court, but when I am dealing with an institution like a bank or an insurance company, when I cannot identify a person who is 'my neighbour,' then the situation becomes different. I can feel free to pursue my rights in court. This is analogous to Paul appealing to Caesar, who had established a good judicious system, when he had a legitimate conflict with the administrators of the Roman Empire. (See Acts 25)

Instead of thinking about taking legal action, think about the process for reconciliation as laid out in Matthew 18:15-17. "If your brother sins against you, go and tell him his fault, between you and him alone. If he listens to you, you have gained your brother. But if he does not listen, take one or two others along with you, that every charge may be established by the evidence of two or three witnesses. If he refuses to listen to them, tell it to the church. And if he refuses to listen even to the church, let him be to you as a Gentile and a tax collector." This gives us a four-step process to follow.

First of all, go the person privately. Then, if that does not provide an outcome, take others along with you. Then, if that does not work, go to arbitration. When dealing with believers, you could involve the church, or otherwise connect with a trade body to mediate. If that does not provide a suitable result, then you could resort to legal means.

Chapter 6: Financing the Business

An important aspect of God's role in our work is to provide sufficient finance. He can sometimes provide in unexpected ways. Can you believe that He will provide what is necessary to finance His work? "But seek first the kingdom of God and his righteousness, and all these things will be added to you." (Matthew 6:33)
Financing through equity, either through savings or external investment, is preferable.

Can we look to the Lord first, before turning to banks for loans? Can we find people to invest in the business and share the risk? Can I use business assets as collateral instead of personally guaranteeing the loan? Standing as personal guarantor for a loan is very risky and to be avoided.

There are two guiding principles: share the risk and avoid bondage!

The Bible gives clear standard to believers to avoid debt. "Just as the rich rule the poor, so the borrower is servant to the lender." (Proverbs 22:7) We want to serve God and not the lender! This principle was established with God's chosen people. ""If you fully obey the LORD your God and carefully keep all his commands that I am giving you today, the LORD your God will set you high above all the nations of the world. You will experience all these blessings if you obey the LORD your God: The LORD will send rain at the proper time from his rich treasury in the heavens and will bless all the work you do. You will lend to many nations, but you will never need to borrow from them." (Deuteronomy 28:1,2 & 12)

If God owns the business, He will provide for its needs. God can do this in unexpected ways and wants us to turn to Him for wisdom and provision in financing our business. Remember, He wants us to maintain our freedom, being independent from the world and dependent upon Him, as we design the financing of the company

I am sure He can enable us to finance all transactions and meet all obligations to those dependent on the business.

I was CEO of a company providing services to the European Space Agency (ESA). This company was set up by the owner, an American, who used to work for NASA. In the US, he earned a lot of money, but through illness and bad investments lost everything. He was married to a Dutch wife, and they decided to move back to Holland. He wanted to start a business, but had decided that, as a Christian, he would not borrow money from a bank. He got a chance to compete for a contract and was awarded the business. Because he would not take a loan to start the business, he asked ESA to pay the contract in advance which would enable him to start the business and employ people. This was unheard of, but the Agency surprisingly agreed. This was a great example of the Lord providing in expected ways!

Can you believe that the Lord will provide when you earnestly seek the priority of the Kingdom and conduct business His way?

When taking on a loan to finance the business, I have found the 5 C's to be helpful.

- Capacity … do I have the staff to manage the business, sufficient administrative or technical capacity?
- Cash Flow – can my business repay the loan I am requesting out of my projected cash flow?
- Capital – what does my balance sheet look like? Do I have saleable assets in the business to cover the loan if necessary?
- Collateral – what assets do I have to make available to secure the loan? Will this affect my family or the business in a negative way?
- Credit – how have I been able to handle any personal obligations required?
- Conditions – are the current and anticipated business and market conditions conducive to taking on a loan? A big problem with debt financing is that we do not know what future business conditions will look like. Debt financing presumes on the future and not on God's promises! "You who say, 'Today or tomorrow, we will go to this or that city, spend a year there, carry on business and make money.' Why, you do not even know what will happen tomorrow… Instead, you ought to say, 'If it is the Lord's will, we will live and also do this or that'" (James 4:13-15)

When financing the business through loans, we could do well by progressing through three stages.[50]

Stage 1. The owner of the business must guarantee the business debt.

When you are launching a business or it's not financially strong, lenders generally require you to personally guarantee its debt. When you personally endorse a debt, you pledge all of your assets as collateral. Many people personally guarantee business debts and don't realize that as long as the debt exists, everything they own is at risk. Proverbs 22:26-27 paints this word picture: "Do not be among those who give pledges, among those who become guarantors for debts. If you have nothing with which to pay, why should he take your bed from under you?"

Stage 2. The business is strong enough to borrow without the owner's guarantee.

We want to challenge you to work toward eliminating the need to personally guarantee business debts. When communicating with a lender, make certain the lender understands that the only security for the debt is the business and anything else you are pledging as collateral.
You have the option of paying the debt in one of two ways: (1) in cash or, (2) with the business and the assets you have pledged as collateral. The lender has a decision to
make. Do I feel good enough about the business and the collateral to loan the money? This eliminates risking all of your other assets. You are no longer slave to the lender.

Stage 3. The business is strong enough to borrow without guaranteeing the loan.

An example of this type of loan would be a well-established real estate investment company that buys an apartment complex and invests enough cash in it that a lender feels comfortable with the complex being the only security. This is the ideal way to borrow. You pledge the money you invested in an asset and the asset itself without risking the business or your other financial assets.

Equity financing, such as venture capital and publicly traded stock, shares the risk with the business. There is no need for personal guarantees and the financiers get a good return on their investment. Many times, investors can get involved in the business. However, one should be careful that venture capitalists, who do not share the owner's goals and values, destroy the company's purpose - to glorify God!

It is important not to take supplier financing without prior knowledge and cooperation of the supplier. This amounts to a deception which does not glorify God. "You shall not steal; you shall not deal falsely; you shall not lie to one another." (Leviticus 19:11)

Other biblical financing methods are available, such as renting or leasing. They all function by the same biblical principles: share the Risk and avoid personal bondage.

Chapter 7: Becoming Debt Free

Debt is discouraged throughout the Bible. Read the first portion of Romans 13:8 from several Bible translations: "Owe no man anything" (KJV). "Let no debt remain outstanding" (NIV). "Pay all your debts" (TLB). "Owe nothing to anyone" (NASB). "Keep out of debt and owe no man anything" (AMP).

Many people think borrowing is inevitable and haven't developed a strategy for their businesses and lives to become debt-free. And as we all have seen, the more debt businesses are encumbered with, the more vulnerable they are to an economic downturn. I have known so many business owners so burdened down with debt, that they have neither energy or inclination to get involved with Kingdom work.

The Lord has called us to be free - free from worry and anxiety which debt often brings - free to serve the Lord and our neighbours with everything we are and have. "For you were called to freedom, brothers. Only do not use your freedom as an opportunity for the flesh, but through love serve one another." (Galatians 5:13

The goal is D-Day - DebtFree Day - when your business or you personally become completely free of debt. I have encouraged many businesspeople to set this goal and work towards it step by step. If we know the Lord wants us to become debt free, then we also know He will give us the resources to achieve the goal. The Lord never, ever, gives a command or principle without giving us the means to carry these out!

When mountain climbers scale a steep face of rock, they often use a technique called "tying the knots." They will climb about ten feet, hammer a spike securely in the rock, and tie their supporting rope to the spike. They do this as a safety precaution. If they slip and fall, they will fall no farther than ten feet and are usually unharmed. However, if the climbers don't tie the knots, a slip can mean serious injury or even death.

The concept of tying the knots is applicable to business and personal debt. When you pay off the debt on an asset, tie the knot! Try not to encumber the free and clear asset in case a financial slip occurs.

A story from the Bible gives us the steps to take to get out of debt.

In 2 Kings 4:1-7, we read how God helped a widow. He can help you in the same way! "Now the wife of one of the sons of the prophets cried to Elisha, "Your servant my husband is dead, and you know that your servant feared the LORD, but the creditor has come to take my two children to be his slaves." And Elisha said to her, "What shall I do for you? Tell me; what have you in the house?" And she said, "Your servant has nothing in the house except a jar of oil." Then he said, "Go outside, borrow vessels from all your neighbours, empty vessels and not too few. Then go in and shut the door behind yourself and your sons and pour into all these vessels. And when one is full, set it aside." So she went from him and shut the door behind herself and her sons. And as she poured they brought the vessels to her. When the vessels were full, she said to her son, "Bring me another vessel." And he said to her, "There is not another." Then the oil stopped flowing. She came and told the man of God, and he said, "Go, sell the oil and pay your debts, and you and your sons can live on the rest."

1. The first and most important step is to pray. The widow called out for help. Seek the Lord's help and guidance in your journey toward Debt Free Day! He can act immediately, as in the case of the widow, or slowly over time. In either case, prayer is essential.

2. Then Elisha asked what the widow already had 'in her house.' God always uses what we have to start off the process. The widow only had a little oil. God starts off with what we place into His hands, however small. He is able to multiply what we give to Him - like the small boy who brought his lunch to feed over 5000 men and women. The disciples were looking to a human solution and came up against a brick wall with an insurmountable financial problem.

3. The widow needed to assess her assets! She had sons to help her work. She has neighbours to lend containers. What assets can you out to work? Then examine every asset in your company or personal belongings to determine if there is anything you could sell to pay down debt more quickly.

4. Elisha told her to 'shut the door.' We should shut the door to any new borrowing. We should sit down and make a realistic assessment of our financial situation, list the debts, and make a new financial forecast, based on what we need to do to increase capacity tor repayments. Ask these two questions about every spending category in your business or

> personal life: Do we need this? If so, can we do it less expensively? The more profitable the business, the quicker you can pay off the debt. Or, in your personal life, the more money is available, the quicker you can pay off the debt.
>
> 5.   The lady and her sons had to work. Not only to package the oil, but also to sell in het marketplace.

As businesses begin to accelerate debt repayment, the Lord is blessing their faithfulness. Even if you can afford only a small monthly prepayment of your debt, do it. The Lord can multiply your efforts.

Snowball your way out of debt, and here's how. In addition to making the minimum payments on all your debts, focus on paying off the smallest debt first. The reason I recommend paying off the debt with the lowest balance first is simple; getting out of debt can be challenging, and we all need to be encouraged by seeing the balance go down and finally disappear.

After the first debt is paid off, apply its payment toward the next smallest one. After the second debt is paid off, apply what you were paying on the first and second toward the third smallest. That's the snowball in action.

This can be exciting as you see the balance really start to drop. So where do you start? List your debts in order with the smallest remaining balance first. If you are disciplined and already making progress on paying off debt, you may choose to focus on paying off the higher-interest-rate debts first, even if the balances are larger.

One important step toward your company or personal life becoming debt free is to stop borrowing more money as soon as practical. If your business depends on credit, ask the Lord for His creativity, direction, and wisdom to eliminate the necessity of continued borrowing.

On October 29, 1941, Winston Churchill, Prime Minister of England, gave a school commencement address. World War II was devastating Europe, and England's very fate as a nation was in doubt. Churchill stood and said,

"Never give in. Never give in. Never, never, never-in nothing, great or small, large or petty-never give in except to convictions of honour and good sense."

So, I want to encourage you to never give up in your effort to get out of debt. It may require hard work and sacrifice, but the freedom is worth the struggle. Remember, it's on God's heart for you and your business to become debt free.

In bankruptcy, a court of law declares a person or business unable to pay its debts. Depending on the type of bankruptcy, the court may allow the debtor to develop a plan to repay the creditors or the court will distribute the debtor's property among the creditors as payment for the debts.

Should a godly person declare bankruptcy? The answer is generally no. Psalm 37:21 tells us, "The wicked borrows and does not pay back, but the righteous is gracious and gives."

However, in our opinion, bankruptcy is permissible under two circumstances:

• If a creditor forces a person into bankruptcy, or

• If the debtor's (or his family's) emotional health is at stake due to an inability to cope with the extreme financial pressure.

After bankruptcy, seek counsel from an attorney to determine how it is legally permissible to repay the debt. Make every effort to repay the debt. For a large debt, this may be a long-term goal that is largely dependent on the Lord's supernatural provision of resources

Chapter 8: Setting Right Prices

I learned early on my business career that a customer does not buy from me because my products are so technically good, or of a very high quality. They only buy if it contributes towards their goals - if it constitutes value for them. The price should reflect the value to the customer, not merely the cost plus profit.

Value-based pricing is determined by how much value your customers attach to your product. A good idea of this value can be achieved by researching competitive products.

1. What is on offer to the customer?
2. Does one product offer more than another?
3. Do the products differ in effectiveness?
4. Do I deliver extra service, delivery or guarantees?

We can determine value by listening to the customer, asking what their goals and expectations are, what their problems are and what they hope to achieve.

A key to maintaining a good price structure is to understand your product quality and service levels and how your offerings stack up against the competition. Establish your pricing structure and hold your line, after you have researched pricing and know you are competitive.

A negotiating tactic used by some was summed up by King Solomon who wrote, "The buyer haggles over the price, saying, 'It's worthless,' then brags about getting a bargain!" (Proverbs 20:14)

We can respond to our customer's objections by pervading evidence of quality and value. Resist the temptation to retreat on a price you believe is competitive and fair. If you are being talked down, ask for evidence, it's OK to be open to new information, but don't respond to jut a lot of words and a strong buyer. Otherwise, your profit margin will be eroded.

One time a salesperson pressed me for a lower price to quote a potential customer on freight costs. I reviewed our cost and price structure and said we were quoting the lowest price possible. Three times the salesperson came back to me pressing for the lower price, I finally said, "Look I can't cut the price, they will just need to ship with our competitor." The salesperson responded, "they would, but the other shipping company doesn't have space." I explained to the salesperson, "the customer needs to decide, use us now at our price, or wait for three weeks and save a few dollars. There is a price for the better service."

Holding pricing firm when you're right will maintain your profit margins.

It is vital that we get to know your customers to make right prices. King Solomon wrote, "Know well the condition of your flocks and pay attention to your herds" (Proverbs 27:23 NASB). In business, your customers are your flock. A petrol station in a neighbourhood with repeat customers, may want to keep prices lower on impulse products like sweets and drinks to encourage more stops. Increasing sales of those extra items will enhance revenues and build up the bottom line. A station on the motorway would do well to raise prices on convenience goods, increasing profit margin, without affecting volume sold.

Another principle is to know your competitors well. Be aware of how your products, customer service, and prices stack up against the competition. Moses sent out spies to check out the opposition (Numbers 13:2), and so should you. If your prices are too low, you may be leaving money on the table and struggling to cover your expenses. At the same time, high prices will often drive customers away. Determine realistically how your service or product is different from the competition, and then determine if you can and should charge more for superior service, or if you need to cut prices to attract more business.

Matching a competitor's price is wise only when there is little difference to the customer in location, quality, or service. A small coffee shop offering specialty coffees and entourage at a higher price than, a fast-food chain. If the small café were to try to match prices with the fast-food chain, the result would be little gain in business but a large loss in revenue. Customers are willing to pay more when they perceive that they are receiving something more of value. In the petrol business, price and location are the key factors. Regardless of appearance, a petrol station will attract few customers if their price is five cents higher than the place across the street.

Many retailers use a standard markup approach to setting prices, adding the same percentage to every item. Although this is an easy approach, it often fails to yield the best results. Consider keeping prices lower on items that customers buy regularly and take a higher margin on products that are likely to be an impulse buy. You will keep your volume moving with sharp pricing on the faster-moving products, but you'll also increase your profit margin on slower moving merchandise.

Price discrimination is setting a price on one service lower to attract customers and giving them the offer to buy more product at a higher margin. This sounds negative, but it doesn't have to be. A cinema sold tickets at a lower price and offered a range of other items like popcorn, booklets, sweets at higher profit levels. This gave families the opportunity to enjoy the film, while not having to spend more on other stuff if they didn't want to.

Some companies add surcharges to boost revenue. For example, airlines charge more for the best seats and for checking baggage. Many hotels charge extra for Internet connections, room safes, and room service. That way, customers who desire added services pay more, instead of everyone. Based on the additional work or overhead invested in customers who require more service and attention, businesses can justify charging different prices. But charging different prices to different customers for the same product or level of service is wrong. Moses wrote, "You shall not have in your house differing measures, large and small" (Deuteronomy 25:14 NASB).

A dry-cleaning business charged a price which included pickup and delivery. The owner soon discovered that he was losing money on jobs with only one small item. To counter this, he added a delivery charge for smaller orders to offset his cost of providing the service and offered a discount to customers who sent in four or more items to clean. Smaller orders became more profitable, and more business was achieved with customers who had more to clean and they were happy with the reduced bill.

Chapter 9: Taking or Giving a Bribe

When financial pressures are high, temptation to compromise may, and likely will, come in a very attractive and tempting package. The Bible says clearly that offering or taking bribes is wrong.

Moses said that accepting a bribe stops you from seeing clearly and leads you in the wrong direction. "And you shall take no bribe, for a bribe blinds the clear-sighted and subverts the cause of those who are in the right." (Exodus 23:8)

The wise Solomon stated, "The wicked accepts a bribe in secret

to pervert the ways of justice. Surely oppression drives the wise into madness, and a bribe corrupts the heart." (Proverbs 17:23 & Ecclesiastes 7:7) A bribe will corrupt your heart and taking a bribe in secret will pervert justice.

When you really need the sale, and accepting a bribe seems so simple, your faith and integrity are being tested. When being confronted with bribery, it is your opportunity to

make a stand, to obey God, even at great personal cost.
Do you want to be able to see God's ways clearly, to keep on track doing business God's way, and to allow God to demonstrate His justice through you? Never, ever take or give a bribe.

There was a time in our business when 80% of the five-year contracts we held at our major customer were ending and needed re-competing. This was a very large part of our total business and if we could not win the contracts again, our business would be in serious trouble. Our customer was an institution which had a strict written policy that no bribes were ever permissible. However, we knew that a major competitor was offering incentives to our customers to grant them the lucrative contracts. Our customer told us and wanted us to give some incentive for him to grant us the business. This was a tough time. We prayed about it and concluded that, because God owned our business, He would never let Himself get involved in bribery. We declined the offer and submitted our proposal. During the contract evaluation process, we learned that the contracts officer had been terminated due to corruption, and that the customer had learned about the offer of bribes. That competitor was disqualified from the process.

Have you ever been confronted with bribery? Can you take a stand for the Lord and His standards of goodness? Remember, He is the owner. If the company has to lose business due to corruption, then it is His loss, and He will deal with it in His way!

Extortion

Extortion is something different. Bribery and extortion do have many characteristics in common, both are offences and involve transactions which influence one of the parties. Extortion involves obtaining items of value or services through the practice of forcing another party to act in an involuntary manner.

I remember travelling with some aid workers into Romania during the cruel rule of the communist dictator Ceausescu. When crossing the border, the armed guards asked us politely to leave behind some electronic goods, otherwise we would not be allowed to proceed. The leader of our party gave over a pack of batteries and some money. I was surprised at the bribes. Later, the leader explained - 'no, that wasn't a bribe, it was extortion. Without giving them something, we would not be allowed to enter the country."

Extortion involves threats and misuse of power. The origin of the English word 'extortion' comes from the Latin 'torquier', which means 'to twist' to extract something. This implies pressure exerted to surrender something to someone with no right to it.

Taking advantage of the weak and poor is detestable in the Lord's sight - be sure He will act against them! "The people of the land have practiced extortion and committed robbery. They have oppressed the poor and needy and have extorted from the sojourner without justice. And I sought for a man among them who should build up the wall and stand in the breach before me for the land, that I should not destroy it, but I found none. Therefore, I have poured out my indignation upon them." (Ezekiel 22:29-31)

Hwa Yung, a writer on the topic of bribery from Malaysia, wrote, "Some wisdom is needed because the line between a gift and bribe is not always clear, especially in non-western cultures. The law must say that bribing is illegal, but social customs may require the giving of some favour. Many questions do not realise that the tension surrounding this complex issue was also felt in the Old Testament.

For example, and six references to bribery in the book of Proverbs, three condemn it (15:27, 17:23, 22:16), but three others show it in positive terms. (17:8,18:16, 21:14)
More importantly, every condemnation of bribery in the Bible it's directed either of those should practice it to pervert injustice, or those who used to positions of power to oppress others, especially the poor. We do not find a single condemnation of those who have to pay because they are in a position of weakness and are forced to do so. In the Old Testament there is a difference between a poor person who gives a gift in order to avoid injustice and the rich who uses power to exploit the poor. The powerful and the powerless are not judged by the same standard but by the relationships and intentions of the situation." 51

As followers of Christ, we represent the being and nature of God in the marketplace. Deception can never be a part of this. Bribery it's not an option for a believer. However, we need to be prepared to answer the many reasons the world will give in favour of bribery and be prepared to pay the cost of not getting involved and bribery.
We should never use bribes to do Gods will.

Chapter 10: Giving From the Business

Gary Grant calls himself "The Entertainer." He is managing director and founder of this chain of toy stores across the UK. The chain of stores is called "The Entertainer". And is UK's largest independent toy retailer, operating 149 stores with revenues of over GBP 140 million, employing between 1500 and 2000 people, depending on the season.

As well as giving away 10% of profits, The Entertainer staff are encouraged to join a payroll giving scheme to give to a charity of their choice.

The Entertainer has the highest employee uptake of Payroll Giving on the high street with 50% of his employees giving. He says: "We encourage our staff to be generous and offer a Payroll Giving scheme to make it really easy. Staff just select a charity of their choice, tell us how much every month and it's all done for them. It's a really easy tax-efficient way of giving. I would encourage employers to lead from the front, to promote it, and you'll be staggered just how many staff will thank you for making Payroll Giving such an easy thing to do." [52]

Also, the company's Pennies scheme means customers can round up their purchase price to give to charity. In 2016, The Entertainer staff and customers donated £1.6 million to children's charities. Customers are prompted by the card machine, website or app checkout to donate a few pennies. It's a yes or no choice, and neither Pennies nor the chosen charity receive any personal data. It is a good example of how technology is making giving easier.

"Working with Pennies has been a dream," says Gary, "this has exponentially increased the amount of money we are capable of collecting… to give to charities." [53]

Giving honours God! "Honour the Lord with your wealth, with the first fruits of all your crops; then your barns will be filled to overflowing, and your vats will brim over with new wine." (Proverbs 3:9,10) To honour God means to give Him the place and position due. That is the first place.

What is a business tithe and what portion of a business' income does it represent? The question of tithing from a business income, as opposed to personal income, is a difficult one for even the most committed businessperson. If many businesses tithed a tenth of their gross income, they would seemingly have a loss. However, it is our dependence on debt and, consequently, high interest payments that make a tithe seem impossible. When the government requires a tenth of total income, the funds will be found. Honouring the Lord with our wealth as a business, I have taken to mean giving the Lord the first tenth of our increase in wealth from one year to the next. This is the profit made, plus what we were able to reserve for future investments. A business' increase is best determined by your profit/loss statement and your balance sheet. A friend of mine tithes from the increase in his assets such as machines, trucks and other equipment.

I believe that the Tithe, a 10%, is the minimum standard of what is due to the Lord, as the rightful owner getting is share first. "Will a mere mortal rob God? Yet you rob me. But you ask, 'How are we robbing you?' In tithes and offerings. Bring the whole tithe into the storehouse, that there may be food in my house. Test me in this,' says the Lord Almighty, 'and see if I will not throw open the floodgates of heaven and pour out so much blessing that there will not be room enough to store it." (Mal 3:8,10)

The great thing about the Tithe is that honouring the Lord on our part brings with it protection for the business. It breaks the power of the competitor, mammon, called by Malachi, 'the devourer.' "I will prevent pests from devouring your crops, and the vines in your fields will not drop their fruit before it is ripe,' says the Lord Almighty. (Mal 3:11)

The concept of offering the 'first fruits' was a recognition of God's provision. "We also assume responsibility for bringing to the house of the Lord each year the first fruits of our crops and of every fruit tree."(Nehemiah 10:35)

Our company purposeful placed 10% of our shares into a charitable trust, which was set upon to benefit children in Africa - the HE Space Operations Children's Trust. We wanted to make sure that the company, if sold, should continue to give a tithe to the charity. We invited staff and customers to give to this charity and organised some events to help raise funds for the purpose of the Trust.

In the final analysis, we are not actually giving to God, but merely returning to Him what He provided in the first place! When David was preparing for a huge building project of the Temple, he gathered large quantities of materials needed from the people, and also grace am enormous offering from his own assets. Je acknowledged humbly, "But who am I, and who are my people, that we should be able to give as generously as this? Everything comes from you, and we have given you only what comes from your hand."(1 Chronicles 29:14)

Chapter 11: When the Stream Runs Dry ...

Sometimes we get into situations where the cash flow starts to dry up, customers leave us or don't pay on time; more money goes out than comes in.

God can bless us just as much by withholding His provision, as well as He can by providing. He uses situations in which He withholds his provision to lead us, to form us, to warn or discipline us. A crisis is God's way of teaching us to how to deal with problems and is our opportunity to focus on Biblical truths and to experience God at work in overcoming such problems. Problems are opportunities for growth!

I remember the bank calling me to say that we were at the limit of a credit line which was completely financed by factoring our receivables. We needed more cash to finance a planned expansion, but this was not forthcoming, despite our prayers for His provision.

We decided to fast and ask God for an answer. It turned out that our market assessment for our planned expansion was incorrect and demand was decreasing. We were just too optimistic about the profitable sales we were expecting. Our focus was too much on money and not on business continuity. We realised that the Lord was protecting us by withholding His provision.

When cash is tight, and you have difficulty paying invoices or making investments, do you spend time asking the Lord for His reasons for withholding His provision so that you can learn from the situation?

Why could God withhold his provision? Here is a list of possible questions to ask.

1.   Is He wanting to take us to a higher level in knowing and rusting Him? It is much harder to trust the Lord when we are experiencing tough times. Th Lord has a purpose in allowing tough times, as Joseph explained to his family, who has seriously mistreated him. "As for you, you meant evil against me, but God meant it for good, to bring it about that many people should be kept alive, as they are today." (Genesis 50:23)

2.   Are we making business decisions based on what scripture tells us? Let is be like the believers in Berea. "Now these Jews were more noble than those in Thessalonica; they received the word with all eagerness, examining the Scriptures daily to see if these things were so." (Acts 17:11)

3.   Have I been unfaithful with what he has entrusted to me? Faithfulness in handling money is, according to Jesus, a condition for being entrusted with more. "If then you have not been faithful in the unrighteous

wealth, who will entrust to you the true riches? And if you have not been faithful in that which is another's, who will give you that which is your own?" (Luke 16:11,12) I find this a very challenging tonight. The measure in which the Lord will trust is with what He calls 'true riches', will be determined by how faithful we are in handling money - His way!

4.   Is He protecting me by foreseeing that in allowing us what we ask for, we might be unfaithful or dishonest in our dealings? Paul said that everything is permissible for us but not all things are helpful. (1 Corinthians 6:12)

5.   Is God withholding something from me because He wants something better for me? Borrowing can often stop God providing in a special way. I remember when I left business to work for Christian business movement. My income was not certain. I needed a car and planned to take a personal loan. However, my wife encouraged me to wait and pray about my need. Not long after, I was given a car by a member of our organisation who know I wanted one. A Mercedes 300D, which I could never have afforded!

6.   Is God withholding something from me because of sin my life? "It's your sins that have cut you off from God. Because of your sins, he has turned away and will not listen anymore." (Isaiah 59:1-2)

7.   Am I convinced that this project is God's will for me? Am I prepared to strive for this in prayer and fasting? "Look here, you who say, "Today or tomorrow we are going to a certain town and will stay there a year. We will do business there and make a profit." How do you know what your life will be like

tomorrow? Your life is like the morning fog—it's here a little while, then it's gone. What you ought to say is, "If the Lord wants us to, we will live and do this or that." Otherwise you are boasting about your own pretentious plans, and all such boasting is evil." (James 4:13-16)

8. Am I taking too many risks by taking on too much credit or getting involved with people whom I don't entirely trust? Is my ambition stronger than my acceptance of God's sovereignty over the situation? (Proverbs 22:7)

9. Do I have enough management and business talent to handle this injection of capital? If not, what skills or people do I need to bring in to deal with it? Remember that amassing riches without the ability to properly handle them can seriously damage us. (Matt 25:11)

It is not so difficult to live with plenty - but it is tough to live and work when we haven't enough to pay the bills! However, the Lord wants us to know how to live in want for certain periods and be content with 'not enough' so we can learn to trust Him. How can we learn to be content in all things if we cannot be content in very troubling times? "Not that I am speaking of being in need, for I have learned in whatever situation I am to be content. I know how to be brought low, and I know how to abound. In any and every circumstance, I have learned the secret of facing plenty and hunger, abundance and need." (Philippians 4:11,12) The secret is not such a secret really, because the answer is given in the next sentence! "I can do all things through him who strengthens me."

In all situations, whether in plenty or in want, we should give thanks to God, because this honours God, and He will open a door for Him to show us His solutions! One of my favourite Bible verses is Psalm 50:23. "The one who offers thanksgiving as his sacrifice glorifies me; to one who orders his way rightly I will show the salvation of God!"

Chapter 12: Financial Planning

What is faith financial planning? Planning our finances is a partnership with God, and we are told that "whatever does not proceed from faith is sin" (Romans 14:23). So, what is faith? Again, the Bible tells us, "Now faith is the assurance of things hoped for, the conviction of things not seen" (Hebrews 11:1).

Faith financial planning has everything to do with an eternal perspective, planning our finances to have the most eternal impact. "And without faith it is impossible to please him, for whoever would draw near to God must believe that he exists and that he rewards those who seek him" (Hebrews 11:6). Financial faith planning is drawing near to God and planning for the

eternal reward.

Most financial plans are based on what has happened in the past. For a Christian entrepreneur, a strategic financial plan should be made on the basis of what God's vision for the business is! This is based on faith! God will make his desires for the company known to those who genuinely seek him. A faith-based plan is made on the basis of God's revelation, with the consultation of advisors. God's plan for the business reflects his character and glory! Through this, the entrepreneur realises that through prayer and our relationship with God, he can be a channel through which God's will becomes reality. "I will stand at my watch and station myself on the ramparts; I will look to see what he will say to me, and what answer I am to give to this complaint. Then the lord replied: 'Write down the revelation and make it plain on tablets so that a herald may run with it. For the revelation awaits an appointed time; it speaks of the end and will not prove false. Though it linger, wait for it; it will certainly come and will not delay. (Habakkuk 2:1-3)

Having written goals makes it far more likely that we will be disciplined and maintain good financial habits. Habits take root in our lives when we have a strong "why" motivating them. Goals provide the why, the necessary motivation. In some ways, written goals close the loop with all the other beneficial financial habits we develop.

Knowing why we are doing something via a written goal helps us create a starting point, stay the course, and know when we are done and can look to new goals. Proverbs 29:18 says, "(ESV) Where there is no prophetic vision the people cast off restraint."

Writing goals is a way to clarify the vision God has given us for our lives. Pursuing them provides a pathway and helps us make more confident decisions today.

As followers of Christ, we are privileged to be able to set goals with God's input and vision. One of my favourite verses says "For we are his workmanship, created in Christ Jesus for good works, which God prepared beforehand, that we should walk in them. " (Ephesians 2:10) God has already prepared works for us to do. When we ask Him to speak into our goals, He can move us into those works and allow us the privilege of completing them.

Only a Christian has the ability to set faith goals and ask, "God what do you want me to achieve?" This is a way to experience the hand of God in my financial situation. A faith goal is a statement: "I believe that God is calling me to __________" (fill in the blank). I need to be wholeheartedly committed to internalising and acting on this statement.

I believe goals (1) give direction and purpose, (2) help crystallise thinking, and (3) provide personal motivation. In building confidence that God will direct my steps, it helps to visualise the sequence.
1. My goal setting comes from God.
2. I seek His will and His wisdom.
3. I start to move.
4. He directs my steps.

A financial plan is a description of the financial implementation of God's vision and his goals for the business. Faith planning is based on what God reveals.
"Surely the Sovereign lord does nothing without revealing his plan to his
servants the prophets." (Amos 3:7) God wants to make his plans known and reveals them to those who seek him in prayer.

Develop a faith-based plan through taking time to ask, seek and knock to find out his will! "So I say to you: ask and it will be given to you; seek and you will find; knock and the door will be opened to you." (Luke 11:9)

Plan with the advice of others.
"Plans fail for lack of counsel, but with many advisors they succeed." (Proverbs 15:22) Receiving advice is an

essential aid in evaluating plans and making sure they are healthy. A faith-based financial plan recognises God as the owner of the business, and that he has the assets to pay for what he has ordered! For business owners who are married, planning with your partner is very important. Your spouse may not understand the business details - but she will undoubtably know God and know you. I remember having the privilege of listening to Dr. Frits Philips, grandson of the founder of the Philips Electronics corporation speaking. On this topic he said, "He who does not ask his wife for advice misses half of God's wisdom! "He based this on the verse 1 Peter 3:7 where it says that marriage partners are "the joint heirs of the grace of life." In other words God peaks to marriage partners equally, but in different ways.

In setting faith financial goals, it is important to regularly evaluate these goals according to the Lord's continuing revelation. The heart of man plans his way, but the LORD establishes his steps." (Proverbs 16:9) It is only when we are carrying out what we consider to be the Lord's plans will these either be established … or not. Remain flexible and willing to change course if needed!

Chapter 13: Managing Risks

This presents a tough dilemma for Christians. Naturally, we want to control everything, so that the business will go as we would want it to. However, the unexpected happens, markets change, people change and business changes.

The dilemma is a choice between seeking to control business outcomes by our own efforts and looking to God to work things out for us. In the first case, we run the risk of not trusting God, and in the second case, we run the risk of testing God. Should we accept all risks and trust in the Lord's provisions?

When wanting to protect ourselves from the financial consequences of the business risks we take, we need to realise that the future is uncertain. This is made clear by the advice the apostle James gave, warning us of too much self-confidence. "Look here, you who say, 'Today or tomorrow we are going to a certain town and will stay there a year. We will do business there and make a profit.' How do you know what your life will be like tomorrow? Your life is like the morning fog—it's here a little while, then it's gone. What you ought to say is, 'If the Lord wants us to, we will live and do this or that.' Otherwise you are boasting about your own pretentious plans, and all such boasting is evil." (James 4:13-16)

Financial risk is increasing due to advances in technology, extensive travel, safety and medical issues - not to mention natural disasters. A large portion of assets has been converted from natural assets, such as land and animals, to financial assets, lightning the awareness of financial risk and our need to pool and spread the risks, giving rise to the insurance industry.

Does taking out insurance mean that I am not trusting in the Lord's provision? I believe there is no such effect. Managing finances is a partnership with God, who is ultimately the Owner. He has a part to play, and I have a part to play. My part is to minimise risks where possible. Hs part is to provide the means to do so. When the Lord asked us to take exceptional risks, He will make it very clear to us.

My role is that of a Steward, to take good care of that which has been entrusted to me. This means to anticipate and prepare for future risks. "The prudent sees danger and hides himself, but the simple go on and suffer for it." (Proverbs 22:3)

Jesus told a story of the contrast between a wise and a foolish man. ""Everyone then who hears these words of mine and does them will be like a wise man who built his house on the rock. And the rain fell, and the floods came, and the winds blew and beat on that house, but it did not fall, because it had been founded on the rock. And everyone who hears these words of mine and does not do them will be like a foolish man who built his house on the sand. And the rain fell, and the floods came, and the winds blew and beat against that house, and it fell, and great was the fall of it." (Matthew 7:24-27)

Rain will come - and God, in His omnipotence, often allows excessive, damaging rain to fall on our houses, but He also gives necessary rain for good harvests. On the one hand withholding, "I also withheld the rain from you when there were yet three months to the harvest; I would send rain on one city and send no rain on another city; one field would have rain, and the field on which it did not rain would wither." (Amos 4:7) On the other hand, blessing: "he will give the rain for your land in its season, the early rain and the later rain, that you may gather in your grain and your wine and your oil." (Deuteronomy 11:14)

Does this mean that we should just passive accept whatever comes our way? To accept that God could increase of decrease our assets as He wishes? The wise man in Jesus' parable, built his business on rock, to protect himself against excessive damage. If God, in His sovereignty, wishes to allow assets to be destroyed than no amount of man's preparation could ever thwart His will. The 'rich fool' in Luke 12 stored up much wealth for himself, preparing for an easy retirement, but the Lord stepped in, despite the man's wealth. "But God said to him, 'Fool! This night your soul is required of you, and the things you have prepared, whose will they be?'" (Luke 12:20)

We need to strike a balance between my part and God's part in managing risk. The prudent man of the proverb, and the wise man of Jesu's parable were praised for their actions. However, the wise man did not immediately resort to the "Jerusalem Insurance Company' but sought to minimise the risks by not building on sand but on rock.

We have a tendency to reduce everything to purely

financial terms and turning to insurance could make our efforts to reduce risk not as intense as they should be. As good stewards, we need to do all we can to provide safe and productive work environments, be prudent in making agreements, and caring for material things and the environment. However, on the other hand, insurance shows our care for people.

I can see four areas in which risks can be mitigated by insurance.

Casualty insurance covers the financial loss of an asset, due to accident, or natural disaster, such as flooding.

Liability insurance provides protection against claims resulting from injuries and damage to other people or property.

A third type is formed by pre-paid benefit plans, such as health insurance, provision payments which serve employees and their families.

Lately, there are life insurance and disability insurance, again protecting families from the tough consequences of income loss.

The concept of sharing risk is central to insurance against risk. Often the premiums for insurance can be too expensive to bear. Sharing risk can also be effectively carried out through cooperatives, or associations which are becoming popular for sole proprietors or small businesses. All share to a small extant in the burden of major losses. This echoes the Biblical command to "Bear one another's burdens, and so fulfil the law of Christ." (Galatians 6:2)

The family is God's basic unit for life. Protection of

workers and their families is a God-given necessity for employers to consider in their financial planning. "But if anyone does not provide for his relatives, and especially for members of his household, he has denied the faith and is worse than an unbeliever." (1 Timothy 5:8) I believe that the Christian employer should consider the employees as His 'business family', as members of his household, to care for and protect.

Insurance is a useful tool to use when loss would be excessive to one's capacity to bear. The tool should never be used out of fear but out of faith, in prayer and with the wisdom of trusted advisors. "Where there is no guidance, a people falls, but in an abundance of counsellors there is safety." (Proverbs 11:14)

Chapter 14: Setting Up a Company

An entrepreneur is faced with many decisions not the least of which concern answering questions like, "should I remain a sole proprietor or have a partner - should I start a limited liability company?"

One of the main reasons to start a limited liability company is to shield oneself against personal liability. When entering into buying or selling arrangements as a representative of a limited liability company, does that remove my personal responsibility?

I have seen the limited liability company used as a tool for fraudulent practices. A business sold advertising space in magazines with highly exaggerated data on readership and circulation. He also borrowed heavily from friends to finance the business. When the deceit was discovered, a court case was brought against the business. It was ordered to pay damages and costs. Having no assets or cash, the company was allowed to take bankruptcy and many customers were left cheated. Friends were left without re-payment of their loans. Not long afterwards, the businessman started again. This businessman was using the limited liability company as a tool for deceit and fraud.

In another case, a business imported chemicals from a supplier in Eastern Europe. These chemicals had to be of a very specific composition and quality is they were to be used in food products. The importer received quality certificates, stamped by local authorities. One of the businesses' customers discovered problems with a batch of their products which had been manufactured with the importer's chemicals. On analysis of the problem, it appeared that that specific chemical was contaminated. The importer was sued for damages but stated that a local government had approved the certificates. However, no continuing controls were carried out. Having insufficient assets and liability coverage to cover the costs, the importer had to file for bankruptcy. In this case, a limited liability company protected the importer, as an innocent party.

My personal responsibility as a steward, is never removed. Even if a limited liability company is able to shield you from costs which the company cannot pay, I believe the responsibility to pay what we have ordered remains, even after bankruptcy. I know of many business owners, who after bankruptcy, took steps to pay their employees and suppliers whatever was due. The exemption was paying back institutions like the government, banks or insurance companies which wrote off debts and had no mechanism to receive payments after bankruptcy.

Forming a partnership is different matter. A Biblical principle which is often quoted as an admonishment not to start partnerships with non-Christians is 2 Corinthians 6:14,15. "Do not be unequally yoked with unbelievers. For what partnership has righteousness with lawlessness? Or what fellowship has light with darkness? What accord has Christ with Belial? Or what portion does a believer share with an unbeliever?" The concept of being unequally yoked comes from the practice of two oxen being paired under a wooden yoke to pull equipment. If the two oxen are not balanced in size and strength, do not pull together equally and accept leadership together, then they could get worn down, move off track and become useless tother master.

This is a good example of two businesspeople in an equal partnership, where each has equal authority. They should bear the burden equally, have the same values, accept the same commitments and have the same goals. If they do not - then misalignment occurs, conflict follows and problems multiply.

The Biblical principle refers in the first instance to a Christian being advised not to form a partnership with a non-Christian. In my experience, at some point, one of the parties has to compromise in vision and values - and that is almost always the believer! I have seen may Christian entering into a partnership with people outside the faith, naively believing that they can make it work. It is a rare occurrence. Many times, the reason for forming a partnership is financial. That, in itself, is not a Biblical principle.

However, I would like to extend the Biblical principles of being unequally yoked to two Christians also. In my experience Christians are no better that non-Christians (only better off!) I have experienced partnerships between Christians falling because of different goals and values. In addition, a partnership between two Christians also encompasses their spouses who may have very different expectations from the enterprise!

In starting a partnership, make sure goals, values and expectations are written down and agreed as clearly as possible. Also include an exit clause. This will save a lot of heartache later if the partnership no longer works.

What about if you are in a partnership which isn't working as you would like? If your faith is being compromised, if you cannot follow God's commands in the business, get out - even if you lose some of the business. "if you have trapped yourself by your agreement and are caught by what you said —follow my advice and save yourself, for you have placed yourself at your friend's mercy. Now swallow your pride; go and beg to have your name erased. Don't put it off; do it now! Don't rest until you do. Save yourself like a gazelle escaping from a hunter, like a bird fleeing from a net." (Proverbs 6:2-5) Remember, God's reputation is at stake!

A good Biblical example of a disastrous partnership is that between Kong Jehoshaphat and King Aphasia. "Some time later King Jehoshaphat of Judah made an alliance with King Ahaziah of Israel, who was very wicked. Together they built a fleet of trading ships at the port of Ezion-geber. Then Eliezer son of Dodavahu from Mareshah prophesied against Jehoshaphat. He said, "Because you have allied yourself with King Ahaziah, the LORD will destroy your work." So the ships met with disaster and never put out to sea." (2 Chronicles 20:35-27)

He did not learn from his disastrous alliance with Ahab (18:28-34) or from his father's alliance with Aram (16:2-9). The partnership stood on unequal footing because one man served the Lord and the other worshiped idols. We court disaster when we enter into partnership with unbelievers because our very foundations differ. While one serves the Lord, the other does not recognise God's authority. Inevitably, the one who serves God is faced with the temptation to compromise values. When that happens, spiritual disaster results.

A limited partnership is possible which allows people to invest in a venture and profit from that investment is not a partnership in the Biblical sense. The managing partner generally has full authority, and the investors have limited authority and liability.

It should be noted that working for a non-Christian-led company is not being unequally yoked in a Biblical sense. God calls you to work under the authority of an employer as a subordinate, serving the Lord in this way. (Colossians 3:22-25)

Investing in shares of a business is also not being Biblically yoked - you are merely buying the right to share in the profits or vote on some policies.

Before entering into partnerships, ask: (1) What are my motives? (2) What problems am I avoiding by seeking this partnership? (3) Is this partnership the best solution, or is it only a quick solution to my problem? (4) Have I prayed or asked others to pray for guidance? (5) Are my partner and I really working toward the same goals? (6) Am I willing to settle for less financial gain in order to do what God wants?

Some Questions To Consider

As you have read, the Bible is our guide to God's best practices. "All Scripture is breathed out by God and profitable for teaching, for reproof, for correction, and for training in righteousness, that the man/woman of God may be complete, equipped for every good work." (2 Timothy 3:16)

1. Decisions … plenty to make, every day! In Part Three you can read about 14 of the main areas in which we have to make financial decisions.

    1. Make a quick review of these 14 decision areas.
    1: Paying wages
    2: Being accountable
    3: Paying invoices
    4: Extending Credit
    5: Collecting debts
    6: Financing the business
    7: Becoming debt free
    8: Setting right prices
    9: Taking or giving a Bribe
    10: Giving from the Business
    11: When the stream runs dry
    12: Financial Planning
    13: Managing risks
    14: Setting up a company

    How are you discovering how to apply Biblical principles to these decision areas?

    Which areas, in particular do you need to address from a Biblical perspective?

    How will you set about to tackle the situation you want to correct?

2. Meeting with other Christians can be a great help in discovering God's best practices from the Bible.

> Are you discussing these with other Christians, sharing experiences, insights and praying for one another?

> What have been the consequences of making wrong decisions?

> How have you experienced God doing His part in helping you make the right decisions?

Part Four: How Can I Make Financial Disciples at Work?

In this part, we will look at how we can obey Jesus' commission to 'go, make disciples.' What does this mean and how can we do this in the context of the workplace?

By the way we handle our decisions at work and taking the opportunities to share our faith, we can have a significant, eternal impact on people. Jesus used the topic of money many times when discipling His followers.

At the end of Part Four, you can find some questions for you to consider.

Chapter 1: Go, Make Disciples!

Jesus' gave a commission to his disciples, before leaving them to continue the work He had started. "And Jesus came and said to them, "All authority in heaven and on earth has been given to me. Go therefore and make disciples of all nations, baptising them in the name of the Father and of the Son and of the Holy Spirit, teaching them to observe all that I have commanded you. And behold, I am with you always, to the end of the age." (Matthew 28:18-20)

The verb 'Go' in Jesus' commission is literally "Go … and while going…" This carries the meaning of 'while we are going about our daily business, in work, family or recreation, make disciples.' It is a whole-life commission. It is not just an activity, but a lifestyle.

Using financial situations to disciple people.

Randy Alcorn gave a helpful overview of how Jesus used financial or economic situations to teach important lessons.[54]

1.		Jesus referred to investment in jewels and treasures to illustrate the importance of investing in the Kingdom of God (the parables of the treasure hidden in the field and the valuable pearl: Matthew 13:44-45)

2.		He referred to saving new treasures as well as old treasures to illustrate the importance of storing up both new and old truths (the parable of the owner of a house and his treasures, new and old: Matthew 13:52)

3.		He used indebtedness to illustrate the importance of forgiveness (the parable of the unmerciful servant: Matthew 18:23-25)

4.		He referred to hiring procedures and wage structures to illustrate God's sovereignty and generosity in treating all with equality, forgiving sins, and rewarding people with eternal life (the parable of the workers in the vineyard: Matthew 20:1-16)

5.		He told a story of a fruit farmer who leased his property to illustrate the way the chief priests and Pharisees were rejecting the Son of God (the parable of the tenants: Matthew 21:33-46)

6.		He discussed capital, investments, banking, and interest to emphasise our human responsibility to utilise God's gifts in a prudent and responsible way (the parable of the talents: Matthew 25:14-30; the parable of the ten minas, Luke 19:11-27)

7.		He referred to money lenders, interest, and debt cancellation to illustrate the importance of love and appreciation to God for cancelling our debt of sin (Luke 7:41-43)

8.		He spoke of building barns to store grain for the future, while neglecting to store up spiritual treasures as a very foolish decision (the parable of the rich fool: Luke 12:16-21)

9.		He used architectural planning, building

construction, and cost analysis to illustrate the importance of future planning and counting the cost before we make decisions in building our spiritual lives (Luke 14:28-30)

10.   He used the human joy that comes from finding lost money to illustrate the joy in the presence of angels when a lost soul believes in Christ (Luke 15:8-10)

11.   He used wealth, dividing up the estate, irresponsible spending, and a change of heart to illustrate repentance and forgiveness (the parable of the prodigal son: Luke 15:11-32)

12.   He used bad financial management and dishonest debt reduction to illustrate that sometimes, people are wiser in their worldly realm than honest followers of Christ are in the spiritual realm (the parable of the shrewd manager: Luke 16:1-12)

13.   He contrasted a rich man who died and went to hell with a poor beggar who died and went to heaven to illustrate how wealth and what it can provide may harden our hearts against spiritual truth (the parable of the rich man and Lazarus: Luke 16:19-31)

14.   He contrasted the proud Pharisee who fasted and tithed regularly with the humble tax collector who acknowledged the sin of dishonesty and greed to illustrate that God acknowledges humility and rejects self-exaltation (the parable of the Pharisee and tax collector: Luke 18:9-14)

He used a grain-ripened field and harvesters to illustrate "spiritually ripened hearts" in Samaria and the part the apostles would have in harvesting people's souls (John 4:34-38)

In our human spaceflight services business, our management team looked at all our 80-plus employees as 'disciples.' Although not professing any faith in Christ, they were learning from us, how Jesus would work and do business. They were learning from us, how to put Biblical principles of business into practice, as we went before them demonstrating and utilising these principles daily. They were learning, from us how to resolve conflicts as Christians, how to put others' well-being first. They were seeing how we act when we made mistakes, asking forgiveness in humility. They observed how we handled finances, how we treated suppliers. . Our constant prayer was that we would be given grace to reflect Jesus in all aspects of our business.

We looked at all our employees as 'pre-Christians.' Don't forget that Jesus' disciples were 'pre-Christians' having been with Him, learning from Him,   for over three years before they actually became Christians at Pentecost!

The commission is to make disciples of all nations. The Greek work used is '*ethnos*,' which means a people group, a tribe. Almost like a business or other organisation with people of a similar culture and aims. Collectively, individual disciples of Jesus are called to disciple entire groups of people—that is, to reveal Jesus (the glory of God) throughout all cultures and in all societies. The workplace is a natural arena for making disciples! You spend half of your waking hours with people at work.

As this corporate disciple-making happens in a organisation, the organisation becomes increasingly Christ-centred.

We are to 'baptise them' into the life of the Trinity. In our churches we look at baptism as a one-time act of commitment - which it surely is, and a wonderful one at that. My baptism in church was hugely inspiring and meaningful. However, I believe baptism to be a lifelong activity as I am constantly immersed in the Trinity,   participating in the dynamic relationship between Father, Son, Spirit and myself!

Our disciple-making is not merely evangelism, introducing people to Jesus, but an ongoing process of enjoying the life of the Trinity.

It is like marriage, which is a one-time, wonderful experience, but must be lived out every day, as we get to know one another, growing in love and dedication and becoming one with each other. I have been married for over 50 years and my wife and I are still getting to know one another, still growing in our marriage, working out life's problems together, end enjoying each other.

Jesus' commission to make disciples also gives us the dynamic of disciple-making. It starts with Jesus, is conducted by Him and finishes with Him. It begins with Jesus' authority, which is is given to Him. This word 'authority' is really *exousia* which means power, influence, strength. We make disciples in Jesus' authority and power. The commission ends with a promise of His presence, "I am with you always." His presence in us, working out through us, is the influencing power as we seek to make disciples.
We do not need more, we cannot do with less.

Being good news

The first step to becoming a disciple begins with trusting another person who happens to follow Jesus. Our life should cause others to choose to follow Jesus.

Two guiding principles are of prime importance.
The first is, "We must be Good News before we can share Good News." People must accept the messenger before they can accept the message. Our speech has to originate from a life which demonstrates what we are saying. People can smell hypocrisy from a mile away!
The second principle is, "People don't care how much we know until they know how much we care." Accepting the messenger must come from a loving, caring relationship

which must be built.

Stephen Covey gives this advice from a manager in the workplace.[55] "If your private performance doesn't square with your public performance, it's very hard for me to open up with you. Then, as much as I may want and even need to receive your love and influence, I don't feel safe enough to expose my opinions and experiences and my tender feelings. Who knows what will happen?

But unless I open up with you, unless you understand me and my unique situation and feelings, you won't know how to advise or counsel me. What you say is good and fine, but it doesn't quite pertain to me.

You may say you care about and appreciate me. I desperately want to believe that. But how can you appreciate me when you don't even understand me? All I have are your words, and I can't trust words.

I'm too angry and defensive—perhaps too guilty and afraid—to be influenced, even though inside I know I need what you could tell me. Unless you're influenced by my uniqueness, I'm not going to be influenced by your advice. "

Sobering advice.

So if we want to be really effective in the habit of interpersonal communication, we cannot do it with technique alone. We have to build skills of empathic listening on a foundation of character that inspires openness and trust. And you have to build what someone called, 'Emotional Bank Accounts' that create an exchange between hearts.

People instinctively appreciate people whose public persona matches their private values.

Influence

Oxford Languages defines influence as "the capacity to have an effect on the character, development or behaviour of someone or something, or the effect itself."[56]

One of the reasons social media influencers are so powerful is that they have carved out a niche for themselves or taken a common issue and approached it from a novel or uncommon way. We need to uncover what it is that makes you unique in order to start making a positive impact on others.

Our uniqueness in the workplace is, of course, our faith in Christ.

So when we are being authentic and shining our the light of Christ consistently, when around others, we're positively influencing them. Why? Because being yourself attracts others to you, and they want to be more authentically them when you're together.

Making disciples in the workplace hinges on our ability to connect with others and formulate deep relationships.

These four key characteristics distinguish someone as a person of influence:[57]

1. **They are intentional.** You can spot someone who is deliberate by how ready for action they are in their work and life. They prioritise what needs to be done throughout the day using efficient scheduling and keeping their sights on a long-term view. They also choose their words with care — when it comes to influencing, words matter.

2. **They connect.** When you come into the space of someone who is influential, you feel included. Sometimes you are asked questions, other times you're offered feedback, all to bring you into the loop – the circle of trust.

This connection reminds you that while they are leading the effort, they do not choose to do it alone. This is why you are much more likely to want to collaborate with them and excited about the possibilities of what you might accomplish together.

3. **They are resilient.** The influential person is aware that things don't always go as planned. When the unexpected happens, they are ready to dig in and find new ways to manage a situation. They are also willing to share this new strategy with their team.

By taking calculated risks and revealing what they are facing, you know they are there for the long haul. The challenges are not debilitating, rather they offer the person of influence a chance to reframe, reboot, and come up with a new plan of action.

4. **They are life-long learners.** In the presence of a person of influence, you're keenly aware that they are one step ahead because of how they constantly choose to grow and learn. They never tell you they've arrived, because they know there's something that will interest them around the corner.

You are drawn to their level of enthusiasm as you see the impact of learning for the sake of learning.

Learning on the job

Most of the people in the world are not cognitive learners; rather, they learn by observation and by experiencing something in their reality.

Today, many people learn by searching the Internet. Data and information are plentiful, but experience and wisdom must be grown. We check Google before asking others.

Harvard educator Fanta-Vagenstein affirms: "Knowledge is learned informally by watching and imitating experts and older, experienced people, through trial and error, and through personal experience acquired over the years ... things are always learned in context." [58]

Does this sound like Jesus discipling His twelve to you?

Most of the world spends a ;large portion of their time at work, or trying to find enough work to make a living. What if we joined the unreached in their jobs — or started businesses to create jobs? Our goal in our space services business was not to maximise profits, but to maximise the number of people we could employ - to bring them under the influence of Christians at work!

The important thing is that the gospel is integrated with how we live wherever life happens, including life in the workplace.

Bill, a business owner, calls it 'walking with God at work.' One of Bill's protégés, adds, "Every day on the factory floor is an opportunity for discipleship." Many of his employees and former employees share about being discipled by this man and his colleagues through their words and actions on the job. They are now followers of Jesus. [59]

These employees embraced Jesus when they saw someone living like Him — with integrity, love, patience, justice, and fairness; ethical behaviour, joy, and excellence. The apostle Paul states it best when he said, "We were well-pleased to impart to you not only the gospel of God but also our own lives...." Paul and his colleagues lived upright, blameless, and encouraging lives (1 Thessalonians 2:8-12). They attracted the unreached to Jesus by how they lived.

Chapter 2: Baptising Them Into the Trinity

In His commission to go and make disciples, Jesus challenges us to "baptise them in the name of the Father and of the Son and of the Holy Spirit."

Baptism is the outward act that symbolises the inward phenomenon of coming to and accepting Jesus Christ as real, as God incarnate, as the sacrificial means by which those who believe in Him can be forever reconciled to God. The purpose of baptism is to give visual testimony of our commitment to Christ. It is the first step of discipleship.

The Greek word for 'baptise' is *'baptizo'* and literally means to 'dip' or to 'immerse.'

The symbolism of baptism is that, just as Christ died and was buried, so the baptised person is submerged under water. Like Christ rose again from beneath the earth, so the baptised person rises again from under the water. Under the water, the believer's old, dead, heavy, suffocating life is left behind. Out of the water, cleansed by the blood of Christ, emerges the believer's new, fresh, purposeful life.

Baptism is like a wedding ring. We put on a wedding ring as a symbol of our commitment and devotion. In the same way, baptism is a picture of devotion and commitment to Christ. A wedding ring reminds us and tells others that we belong to someone special. In the same way, baptism reminds us and others that we are devoted to Christ and belong to Him.

I could not think that baptism is only a one-off occurrence, as wonderful as that may be and is! Just as many people say that getting married was the most wonderful day of their lives, that day is followed by a life-long process of getting to know, love and enjoy one another.

Baptism must also be like that. A one-time commitment, followed by a lifetime of working out your baptism; getting to know, live and enjoy God in all His fulness!

So, what does Jesus mean when He is challenging us to "baptise them in the name of the Father and of the Son and of the Holy Spirit."

I believe He means us to immerse them, completely, into the dynamic life of the Trinity.

The Trinity

A full discussion of the Trinity is out of the scope of this book, but here is a short definition.

We believe that the one God eternally exists in three Persons: the Father, the Son, and the Holy Spirit; and that these three are one God, co-equal and co-eternal, having precisely the same nature and attributes, and worthy of precisely the same worship, confidence, and obedience. [60]

The Bible contains many statements regarding the unity of God. Deuteronomy 6:4 tells us that "the Lord is one." It also speaks clearly about diversity within that unity. For example, in the very first verse of the Bible we are told that "In the beginning, God." The word used for God in Hebrew is '*elohim*,' which is the plural form of the word '*el*.' Elsewhere in the Bible, it is sometimes translated as "gods," referring to heathen deities.

Right from the beginning, in Genesis 1, we have one of a clear statement of unity-in-diversity. "

Then God said, "Then God said, "Let *us* make man in our image, after *our* likeness. And let them have dominion over the fish of the sea and over the birds of the heavens and over the livestock and over all the earth and over every creeping thing that creeps on the earth." (Genesis 1:26)

Created in the image of the Triune God, we are given the privilege to work the earth.

The individual members of the Trinity have different tasks. The Father is the ultimate source or cause of the universe (1 Corinthians 8:6); of divine revelation (Revelation 1:1); salvation (John 3:16-17); and Jesus' human works (John 5:17& 19). The Father initiates all of these things.

The Son is the agent through whom the Father does the following works: the creation and maintenance of the universe (Colossians 1:16-17); divine revelation (John 1:1); and salvation (2 Corinthians 5:19). The Father does all these things through the Son, who functions as His agent.

The Holy Spirit is the means by whom the Father does the following works: creation and maintenance of the universe (Psalm 104:30); divine revelation (2 Peter 1:21); salvation (Titus 3:5; and Jesus' works (Acts 10:38). Thus, the Father does all these things by the power of the Holy Spirit.

We are created in the image of God, and we can imitate God by learning, as disciples, to carry out these roles, as we are gradually taken up into the life of the Trinity.

I have been profoundly influenced in designing work, as a Christian by the writings of Christian Schumacher, in his book, "To Live and Work." He explains how we can imitate God by following the work of the three expressions of God - Father, Son and Holy Spirit. He started with the simple distinction between, 'the work - to work - and working.' God the Father initiates 'the work.' God the Son gives form and body to the work, and the Spirit is working to accomplish the work. Seeing God as Trinity is the compass to understanding discipleship at work. [61]

Helping people to enter into this working relationship of the Father, Son and Holy Spirit, is discipleship.

The work of God the Father is to initiate, plan, originate and envision.

The work of the Son is to execute the plan, give form to the vision, to express everything the vision entails.

The work of the Spirit is to empower, to equip, give skills, judgement and motivation to carry out the work.

Created in the image of God, we can help people to imitate how God works, by leading them into this dynamic relationship to envision the work, execute the work and being empowered for the work. Wether Christian believer or not, work can only be complete and whole if people have the opportunity to envision, execute and be empowered for their work. We will look at each of these three expressions of the work of the Trinity.

Envision

Discipling means to help people in the role of the Father in their lives. This is helping them see a clear picture of what God is planning for them and the work He is calling them to do.

Vision does not come out of brainstorming sessions, positive thinking, or anything we could think up. It comes from revelation of the work God wants doing, changed, organised, built, created.

God already has plans for us. "For I know the plans I have for you, declares the LORD, plans for welfare and not for evil, to give you a future and a hope." (Jeremiah 29:11) He reveals His plans, as the King said to Daniel, "Truly, your God is God of gods and Lord of kings, and a revealer of mysteries, for you have been able to reveal this mystery." (Daniel 2:47)

We need a vision of what the Lord wants done, what His plans for us are, in order to enter into the discipline of participating in God's work. "Where there is no prophetic vision the people cast off restraint, but blessed is he who keeps the law." (Proverbs 29:18)

Vision is always given for a purpose, planned by God. The Lord said to Paul in his encounter with Christ, "But rise and stand upon your feet, for I have appeared to you for this purpose, to appoint you as a servant and witness to the things in which you have seen me and to those in which I will appear to you." (Acts 26:16)

Vision comes through prayer. "Let your work be shown to your servants, and your glorious power to their children." (Psalm 90:16) Vision comes from spending time with Him, as He invites us to, "Come up here, and I will show you what must take place after this." (Revelation 4:1)

It takes a our pure character to see what God envisions

for you. "Blessed are the pure in heart, for they shall see God." (Matthew 5:8)

It requires diligent patience. "And the LORD answered me: "Write the vision; make it plain on tablets, so he may run who reads it. For still the vision awaits its appointed time; it hastens to the end—it will not lie. If it seems slow, wait for it; it will surely come; it will not delay." (Habakkuk 2:2,3)

It requires obedience. As Paul said,""Therefore, O King Agrippa, I was not disobedient to the heavenly vision…" (Acts 26:19)

The vision which God has given us at Compass is that "all people everywhere would faithfully live by God's financial principles in every area of their lives." Just imagine what happens when this vision becomes reality. In business, people come before profits; suppliers are paid on time; employees are given a good, fair wage; a business would have no debt; the business gives away a large part of their profits; co-workers have no personal financial problems which bother them during their work. Etcetera. Just imagine!

That's why financial discipleship at work is so important.

Execute

Discipling means to help people to execute, to carry out the work which God has prepared for them, to do and accomplish His will.

After seeing what the Lord has envisioned for us, and realise the work that He has prepared, we need to go ahead and do it! "For we are his workmanship, created in Christ Jesus for good works, which God prepared beforehand, that we should walk in them." (Ephesians 2:10)

There's a quote I love that says, "Vision without

execution… is just hallucination." [62]People attribute it to everyone from Edison to Einstein. Someone traced it back to an early Japanese proverb. "Vision without action is a daydream," the Japanese proverb goes.

Jesus carried out, and completed the work which the Father had prepared for Him to do. "I glorified you on earth, having accomplished the work that you gave me to do." (John 17:4)

Jesus, as the Son, only did what the Father had envisioned and planned for Him to do. "Truly, truly, I say to you, the Son can do nothing of his own accord, but only what he sees the Father doing. For whatever the Father does, that the Son does likewise. For the Father loves the Son and shows him all that he himself is doing. And greater works than these will he show him, so that you may marvel." (John 5:19)

This cost Jesus significantly, who sacrificed Himself to execute the Father's plan.He emptied Himself to laser-focus on God's plan, no matter what the cost.

He put the Father's interests before His own, He put people before programmes, He loved and served those God brought across His path.

Jesus, "who, though he was in the form of God, did not count equality with God a thing to be grasped, but emptied himself, by taking the form of a servant, being born in the likeness of men. And being found in human form, he humbled himself by becoming obedient to the point of death, even death on a cross." (Philippians 2:6-8)

In the execution of His work to carry out God's plan of salvation, Jesus was very productive. This was not characterised by numbers, but on the way He trained a small number of disciples, who would then become 'fishers of men,' and multiply. Productivity is effectively stewarding your gifts, talents, time, energy, and enthusiasm for the good of others and the glory of God.

"Look carefully then how you walk, not as unwise but as wise, making the best use of the time, because the days are evil." (Ephesians 5:15-16). Our days are filled with good things which distract us from the main task God gives us, to love our neighbour as ourselves, with all that this entails. To serve them to that they can become all God has envisioned for them.

Empower

To disciple means to help people realise and utilise the power of the Holy Spirit in order to get things done.

Jesus was a real human being, which means he grew 'spiritually' by learning to be open to the Spirit. He needed to be empowered from day one with and by the Holy Spirit. If this is true, then it is true that you and I need the Holy Spirit, more so.

Peter explained to the Roman Centurion, Cornelius and his entourage; "You yourselves know what happened throughout all Judea, beginning from Galilee after the baptism that John proclaimed: how God anointed Jesus of Nazareth with the Holy Spirit and with power. He went about doing good and healing all who were oppressed by the devil, for God was with him." (Acts 10:37,38)

Those who wrote the New Testament leave us in no doubt that the Son could what he did, through and only through the power of the Spirit dwelling in Him.

Jesus knew he was being empowered by God's Spirit. For his opening-day sermon in his hometown, Jesus read from the prophet Isaiah; "The Spirit of the Lord is upon me, because he has anointed me to proclaim good news to the poor. He has sent me to proclaim liberty to the captives and recovering of sight to the blind, to set at liberty those who are to proclaim the year of the Lord s favor." (Luke 4:18-19)

The works which Jesus did, not only originated from the Father' vision, but were executed with the power and presence of the Spirit.

Jesus lived his life by the Spirit's power. We need to disciple people in the Spirit, so they can appropriate the power of the Spirit to help them live a life of purpose and impact, an abundant, joyful and victorious life.

The Spirit will empower disciples in a way in which they could not think possible under their own steam.

"See, I have called by name Bezalel the son of Uri, son of Hur, of the tribe of Judah, and I have filled him with the Spirit of God, with ability and intelligence, with knowledge and all craftsmanship, to devise artistic designs, to work in gold, silver, and bronze, in cutting stones for setting, and in carving wood, to work in every craft. And behold, I have appointed with him Oholiab, the son of Ahisamach, of the tribe of Dan. And I have given to all able men ability, that they may make all that I have commanded you." (Exodus 31:2-6)

We see here the work (commanded by God), executing the work (making the beautiful tabernacle in this case) and the empowerment for the work (filled with the Spirit producing ability, skill and knowledge.)

Making disciples is immersing people in all the Trinity can mean for them, so that they can carry out the Lord's plans for them.

Groups

Work is normally not carried out in isolation. We work with others and are partially dependent on them. We need people with complementary skills, talents and resources needed. People collaborate to make a product or provide a service. This is merely a reflection of the work of the Trinity in creation.

The effectiveness of a group of people will also be determined by the way they are able to Envision their work, Execute the plan and be Empowered to do the work.

The disciple can play an essential role by helping the others in the team to work in the same way as the Trinity would work. Remember, discipleship is immersing people in the life of the Trinity. The disciple will grow in helping people in his team of collaborators to carry out the envisioning, execution and empowering roles, as a team.

In what way do the Father, Son and Spirit work together? Of course, in complete harmony and unity, each fulfilling their different roles while complementing each other. It is the ultimate example of 'unity in diversity.'

The glue which hold all this together is love, because we are told; "Beloved, let us love one another, for love is from God, and whoever loves has been born of God and knows God. Anyone who does not love does not know God, because God is love." (1 John 4:7,8)

Imagine the end of a day's sales conference at a large insurance company. The invited keynote speaker gets up and delivers this bombshell: "Everything you've heard so far is not true." Tony Campolo, then professor emeritus of sociology at Eastern University in Pennsylvania, opened his speech with this statement after some power speakers had instructed the audience on how to "set up" clients, push the right emotional buttons, and close the deal. Tony's task was to "psych up" the audience for a last big motivational push. You can imagine the shock when he said, "Everything you've heard so far is not true!" [63]

"People are not things to be manipulated with the right techniques," he said, "not economic objects. They are entitled to love." The audience was enthralled as he made a case to make "love" a verb to be demonstrated daily in the office and the factory.

Yahoo senior executive, Tim Sanders, wrote a book with a great title; "Love: The Killer App!" He writes, "The most powerful force in business isn't greed, fear, or even the raw energy of unbridled competition. The most powerful force in business is love." He gives a powerful definition. Love "is the selfless promotion of the growth of the other." [64]

A business friend described love at work in a very practical paraphrase of 1 Corinthians 13:

"Although I have the communication skills of men and angels and have not love, I sound just like a clanging cymbal. If I can predict business trends and have a total grasp of the latest production techniques, and have the kind of positive thinking that people say is the secret of success but have no love, it really does no lasting good. And although I make all the sacrifices so that there can be better wages for my workers, and make sure they have all the fringe benefits possible and do not show them love, it will still leave them grumbling and discontented. Love teaches me to put up with a lot of things that would ordinarily make me angry, and it makes me into a listening, sensitive person. It keeps me from acting like a big shot and going on ego trips. Love keeps me from being rude to even the lowliest person in the company. It keeps me from demanding that things al- ways be done my way; it keeps me from blowing up at the least little thing. And it prevents me from keeping files on all the mistakes made by people working for me. Love gets no satisfaction out of the failures of others—even when their failures guarantee that I will get a promotion."

Let the dynamic life of the Trinity permeate your entire being, as you are immersed in the presence of the Father, Son and Spirit. This life will pour out of you as you are filled with the life of God and imitate the Trinity at work.

Chapter 3: Discipling in the Workplace

You are where you are by God's assignment, stay there until called elsewhere.

Paul wrote this principle about our work to Corinthian Christians in 1 Cor 7:17-24. This principle is repeated three times in this paragraph:

"Nevertheless, each one should retain the place in life that the Lord assigned to him and to which God has called him." (v. 17).

"Each one should remain in the situation which he was in when God called him." (v. 20).

"Brothers, each man, as responsible to God, should remain in the situation God called him to." (v. 24).

The challenge is to be a disciple where you are called right now. Grow and flourish where you are planted. We have a job to do where God has called us.

Bearing fruit where you are

Mark Greene, former advertising executive and director

of the 'London Institute for Contemporary Christianity' wrote a great booklet called, "Fruitfulness on the Frontline." [65] In this he mentions six ways, 6 M's, in which we can bear fruit at work., which pleases God. I have added a seventh.

- Model godly character.
- Make good work.
- Minister grace and love.
- Mould the culture.
- Be Mouthpieces for truth and justice.
- Be Messengers of the gospel.
- Make disciples

What would these 7 'M's' look like for an plumber?

He would model godly character, keeping his word, arriving on time, being conscientious and working hard.

He would make good work, installing quality systems and repairing broken pipes to last.

He would minister grace and love, reacting quickly to problems, setting a fair price, and be willing to help people who had difficulty paying.

He would mould the culture around his work, developing trust, with pleasant conversations, communicating well, using good language and adhering to his values.

He would be a mouthpiece for truth, refusing tax evasion, and promoting truth-telling, explaining his beliefs, motivations and why he does what he does.

He would be a messenger of the gospel, taking opportunities to share Jesus with customers and suppliers.

He would make disciples, demonstrating Jesus at work, and seeking to help others to know Christ.

Having a spiritual conversation

A spiritual conversation with colleagues at work can

seem daunting for many, and give rise to fear and apprehension.

Maybe you feel you are not ready to answer the questions you fear colleagues will throw at you, or that initiating a spiritual conversation is 'not done' in the workplace. Maybe you expect a hostile attitude toward Christianity from some colleagues. You may be afraid that your example as a Christian disqualifies you. Take heart! The Holy Spirit will help you and give you the words to say! "And when they bring you before the synagogues and the rulers and the authorities, do not be anxious about how you should defend yourself or what you should say, 12 for the Holy Spirit will teach you in that very hour what you ought to say." (Luke 12:11-12)

It does not have to begin with a deep spiritual conversation. You could start someone on a spiritual journey with Jesus just by sharing a cup of coffee with a colleague. You could seek to encourage someone who is having a rough time at work. You could offer a helping hand to a boss or coworker in a stressful situation.

One of my favourite times for sharing something spiritual is on Monday morning. At the coffee break, I ask, "How was your weekend?" "What did you do on your free Sunday?" This opens a door to share what you did at church, what you learned from the Bible.

At work, I almost always kept an opened Bible on my desk. It was a special edition 'Leadership Bible.' This often gave rise to a conversation on what the book was all about!

Listening before talking

The early Greeks had a magnificent philosophy which embodied three sequentially arranged words: ethos, pathos, and logos. These three words contain the essence of seeking first to understand and conducting effective conversations. "Ethos is your personal credibility, the faith people have in your integrity and competency. It's the trust that you inspire, your Emotional Bank Account. Pathos is the empathic side—it's the feeling. It means that you are in alignment with the emotional feelings behind someone's communication. Logos is the logic, the reasoning part of the what we say." [66]

The sequence is important: ethos, pathos, logos—be credible, build a relationship, and then share logically. When starting a discussion, most people, begin with logos, the logic, of their ideas, and put forward] arguments to defend that logic. Without first taking considering ethos and pathos, the discussion will not be fruitful.

Empathetic listening

Habit 5 in Steven Covey's book "The 7 Habits of Highly Successful People," is "Seek first to understand, then to be understood. This needs a shift in our way of approaching people. Most people do not listen with the intent to understand; they listen with the intent to reply. They're either speaking or preparing to speak. They're filtering everything through their own paradigms, reading their autobiography into other people's lives."

Covey says, "When another person speaks, we're usually 'listening' at one of four levels. We may be ignoring another person, not really listening at all. We may practice pretending. "Yeah, aha, right…" We may practice selective listening, hearing only certain parts of the conversation. We often do this when we're listening to the constant chatter of a preschool child. Or we may even practice attentive listening, paying attention and focusing energy on the words that are being said. But very few of us ever practice the highest form of listening, empathic listening. When I say empathic listening, I mean listening with intent to understand."[67]

Seeking first to understand is the key to influencing others. When we understand people, we appreciate them more, and become sensitive to what their needs are.

Being vulnerable

One of the most powerful ways to connect with people is to dare to be vulnerable; to open yourself to others in an honest way. It has been my experience that the extent to which a person will open up to me, is largely determined by the extent to which I will open myself up to him or her.

To be vulnerable is not a weakness, but it is a risk to take. It may be used against us, if the person to whom we show ourselves vulnerable is hoist to us. However in most cases, I have experienced people to be thankful that you dare to show your weaknesses; share your failures and disappointments - after all, you are only human!

I was hugely impacted by a TED talk from Dr. Brené Brown in which she talked about 'the power of vulnerability.' In this talk she said, "vulnerability is the core, the heart, the centre of meaningful human experience. "Vulnerability is the birthplace of love, belonging, joy courage, empathy, and creativity." [68]

People don't want to talk to 'superman,' but to a normal person who goes through the same Scala of experiences and emotions as they.

Discipling your boss.

The first step is to cultivate a trusting relationship with

your boss. Many managers struggle to trust that their teams and subordinates are indeed working as he or she wants and are delivering the expected outcomes in the agreed quality.

We have to develop the art of 'Managing up.' This is the systematic process of working with your boss to obtain the best possible results for you, your boss and your organisation. When you manage upwards, you show leadership on your own part.

We need to ensure our work anticipates our boss's needs and expectations. Clarify what your boss expects from you. Ask direct questions like, "What are your priorities for me?" and "What criteria should I take into account when making decisions?" And find out how your boss prefers to work with you, including how often you two should meet and when they expect you to be reachable by email and phone. Knowing these expectations now could save you headaches in the future.

We should communicate intent and expectations, give regular feedback and deliver on commitments.

The Bible gives some guidelines as to how we should work with our managers, such as the following …

"Bondservants, obey in everything those who are your earthly masters, not by way of eye-service, as people-pleasers, but with sincerity of heart, fearing the Lord. Whatever you do, work heartily, as for the Lord and not for men, knowing that from the Lord you will receive the inheritance as your reward. You are serving the Lord Christ." (Colossians 3:22-24)

"Servants, be subject to your masters with all respect, not only to the good and gentle but also to the unjust.." (1 Peter 2:18)

Only when I have gained the trust of my boss, through my good work and right attitude, will I be given the freedom to speak about faith matters.

Discipling your colleagues

The same pre-requisite of trust is also valid for creating conditions in which we can start a discipling relationship with our colleagues.

In the New testament, we read many times the two powerful words, 'one-another.' This gives a key to opening the door to a growing trust with our colleagues. I recommend substituting your colleague's name in place of the 'one-anothers' as you consider what would happen if you modelled these at work.

- "Do nothing from selfishness or empty conceit; but with humility of mind regard one another as more important than yourselves; do not merely look out for your own personal interests, but also for the interests of others." (Philippians 2:3-4)
- "Be at peace with one another." (Mark 9:50
- "Live in harmony with one another." (Romans 12:16)
- "Let us not pass judgment on one another." (Romans 14:13)
- "So then let us pursue what makes for peace and for mutual upbuilding." (Romans 14:19)
- "Therefore welcome one another as Christ has welcomed you, for the glory of God." (Romans 15:7)
- "Serve one another in love." (Galatians 5:13)
- "Bear one another's burdens, and so fulfil the law of Christ." (Galatians 6:2)
- "With all humility and gentleness, with patience, bearing with one another in love." (Ephesians 4:2)
- "Be kind to one another, tenderhearted, forgiving one another, as God in Christ forgave you." (Ephesians 4:32)
- "Do not lie to one another…" (Colossians 3:9)

- "Comfort one another…" (1 Thessalonians 4:18)
- "See that no one repays anyone evil for evil, but always seek to do good to one another and to everyone." (1 Thessalonians 5:15)
- "Encourage one another . . ." (Hebrews 10:25)
- "Do not grumble against one another, brothers, so that you may not be judged." (James 5:9)
- "Above all, keep loving one another earnestly, since love covers a multitude of sins." (1 Peter 4:8)

I am sure that your colleagues will open up to you, and be willing to explore the reasons and motivations which lie behind your life, when you adhere to these challenges.

Discipling employees

Again, building trust is vital in order to be able to talk with your employees about spiritual matters.

Do I treat my people justly and equally? "Masters, treat your bondservants justly and fairly, knowing that you also have a Master in heaven." Colossians 4:1) (Do I set standards for them which I refuse to keep myself? "Masters, do the same to them, and stop your threatening, knowing that he who is both their Master and yours is in heaven, and that there is no partiality with him." (Ephesians 6:9)

Am I considering the needs of those around me? "Do nothing from selfish ambition or conceit, but in humility count others more significant than yourselves. Let each of you look not only to his own interests, but also to the interests of others. (Philippians 2:3,4)

A wonderful promise which is stated in the Bible, comes out of a situation in which people were being persecuted with high tax burden, placed on them by Solomon. His son Rehoboam was asked to receive this burden on the people and went for advice to some old counsellors. ""How do you advise me to answer this people?" And they said to him, "If you will be a servant to this people today and serve them, and speak good words to them when you answer them, then they will be your servants forever." (1 Kings 12:7)

This gives two ways which will open the door for people to accept us and our teachings. Firstly, to be their servant, seeking their best interests. Secondly, knowing how to answer their questions correctly. Then, they will attach themselves to us.

Being discipled

It takes one to make one! If you want to become a 'make of disciples,' then you need to be discipled yourself.

Look for someone who is older in the faith, with whom you could study the Bible, pray and grow as a believer.

Paul met Christ on the Damascus Road at about the age 33-35, not sooner than about 33 A.D. Taking the fact that his fist missionary journey did not begin until approximately the year46 or 47, this would make Paul a middle-aged man in his late forties. During that time, he spent years alone with the Lord, but was also discipled by Barnabas.

Barnabas' relationship with Paul began when he introduced him to the apostles in Acts 9, but his mentoring relationship started in earnest when Barnabas recruited Paul to help him teach the new followers of Christ in Antioch (Acts 11:25-26). Barnabas guided Paul during his development from a novice follower of Christ to the greatest propagator of the faith in the early church. The mentoring relationship between Barnabas and Paul worked because they each accepted their roles as mentor and mentee and adapted them as they progressed through the mentoring process.

Paul displayed humility by submitting himself in this process. This form of mentoring relationship was most likely not new to Paul. As a Pharisee (Acts 23:6) Paul was accustomed to learning from his elders as he developed as a Pharisee (Galatians 1:14).

Mentoring was a life-style for Barnabas also. Barnabas guided Paul by spending time with him and letting Paul observe him interact with new believers at Antioch (Acts 11), church leaders (Acts 13), and non-believers in their first missionary journey.

Barnabas was truly an 'encourager.' We need to be disciples, mentored by another, more mature believer, who can help and encourage us in our task of making disciples at work.

I have been blessed to have been given many such people to help me in fulfilling the Great Commission to 'go and make disciples.' These have mede a huge impact on my disciple-making. Amongst them are, for example:

Robb-Powrie-Smith, Loughborough, England; "Memorise the Word, so it will always be with you."

Jim Johnston , an accountant from Belfast, Northern Ireland; "The best you can do for someone is to set them free."

Albert Diepeveen, an entrepreneur from Chicago, USA; "You cannot outgive God."

Dr. Ad Guggenbühl, a lawyer from Zürich, Switzerland' "Use all your resources to introduce people to Jesus."

Dr. Siegfried Buchholz, a CEO from Vienna, Austria; "If you think you are leading but no-one is following, you are just taking a walk in the park."

Get a mentor - you will be enriched!

Chapter 4: in a Challenging Environment

Many disciples in secular jobs work in toxic environments where they feel there is no place to share the Gospel. How can they carry out their mission to make disciples in a challenging environment?

There are many biblical examples of God's people working in pagan or hostile environments. David, for example, mentions 'enemies' in at least 53 out of his 75 Psalms. His work was often life-threatening but that was his calling. Our workplace may be tough, but God wants to work through us right there – for as long as we're there.

Jeremiah makes it clear that Babylon, a strange place of exile, is where God wants His people to seek peace and wholeness, not only for themselves but also for the city and the people in it. "But seek the welfare of the city where I have sent you into exile, and pray to the LORD on its behalf, for in its welfare you will find your welfare." (Jeremiah 29:7)

We seek the wellbeing of our organisation, as well as the

salvation of those working in it. We pray for it. To be a disciple of Jesus is to join a movement to change our environment. We contribute to that through our daily tasks which, for the most part, serve the common good in some way.

So the goal for Christians at work is not to share the Gospel without consideration for our surroundings. It is to work well, love our neighbour-colleagues, develop relationships of trust, and to seek to show wisdom through our action and words. This, over time, invariably leads to opportunities to share the difference Jesus can make in their lives.

Working in tough environments

We are more and more secularised every day, and we're living in a post-Christian society. Mary Lowman says, "When you go to work each day, you are likely to be leaving your comfort zone and entering a different kind of world." [69]

In writing to the church in Pergamum, Jesus said—through the Apostle John—"*I know where you dwell, where Satan's throne is. Yet you hold fast my name, and you did not deny my faith.*" *(Revelation 2:13)*. Pergamum was the capital city of Asia, and hosted many temples to different gods. Pergamum was thoroughly pagan, and many Christians were martyred there. Our challenge is to remain true to the Lord even though we may work in Satan's territory

Mary Lowman continues, "There are probably no "temples" erected to pagan gods where you work, but no doubt there is pagan worship all around you. The gods are a bit different today, but they are there:
- The god of materialism
- The god of success
- The god of sexual pleasure

- The god of any kind of pleasure
- The god of the unholy trinity - I me and myself."
(Ibid)

When we feel attacked or challenged at work, it's important to remember that we are not alone. God is with us, and He is fighting for us. We can also take comfort in knowing that we are not the only ones experiencing spiritual warfare. The Bible is full of accounts of God's people overcoming difficulties through His strength and power.

In my work with our contracting company to the European Space Agency, I sensed this spiritual warfare in this environment where scientific materialism was the major philosophy. Looking around the car park at the Agency, I noticed that many cars had bumper stickers with a kind of *'ichthus'* fish. At first glance, you might think of the Christian symbol, but on a close look the fish all had feet, symbolising the evolutionary theories of Darwin!

(One senior executive who told me that Christianity has been surpassed by our scientific knowledge, did have a statue of Gautama Buddha in his office!)

Our prayers were not only for the salvation of our friends at work but also to bind these strongholds of the world's philosophies.

I know of a company which was suffering from what they perceived to be 'spiritual attacks.' They recruited some fellow believers to form an intercessory group to pray for protection for the company and to break the anti-Christian power which was developing. They prayed for insight into the spiritual problems of the company and wisdom to overcome these. The Lord brought healing and restoration to the business.

Paul writes of his time in Ephesus when he was 'fighting

with wild beasts.' (1 Corinthians 15:32) he was not literally a gladiator in the Games, but fighting with spiritual forces. To the believers in Ephesus he said, "For we do not wrestle against flesh and blood, but against the rulers, against the authorities, against the cosmic powers over this present darkness, against the spiritual forces of evil in the heavenly places." (Ephesians 6:12)

When spiritual warfare comes knocking at our door, we must remember our true enemy. We are not fighting against flesh and blood but against spiritual forces of evil. This is why it's so important to be in prayer and have our spiritual armour on at all times.

In order to navigate spiritual warfare at work, we need to be equipped "Therefore take up the whole armour of God, that you may be able to withstand in the evil day, and having done all, to stand firm. Stand therefore, having fastened on the belt of truth, and having put on the breastplate of righteousness, and, as shoes for your feet, having put on the readiness given by the gospel of peace. In all circumstances take up the shield of faith, with which you can extinguish all the flaming darts of the evil one; and take the helmet of salvation, and the sword of the Spirit, which is the word of God, praying at all times in the Spirit, with all prayer and supplication." (Ephesians 6:13-18)

Then Paul goes on to encourage us to persevere, right through these tough times, so that we. Can share the gospel.

"To that end, keep alert with all perseverance, making supplication for all the saints, and also for me, that words may be given to me in opening my mouth boldly to proclaim the mystery of the gospel, for which I am an ambassador in chains, that I may declare it boldly, as I ought to speak." (Ephesians 6:19,20)

Daniel

Daniel, and his three faithful friends, were fully immersed in a pagan culture. They worked hard and succeeded in their work. But they did not adapt their lifestyles or beliefs to the pagan world around them. Their approach was obedient involvement: They stayed involved in the world, while at the same time remaining obedient to God and his principles.

Jesus prayed specifically for his disciples: "I do not ask that you take them out of the world, but that you keep them from the evil one. They are not of the world, just as I am not of the world. Sanctify them in the truth; your word is truth." (John 17:15-17).

Daniel knew the Scriptures and I believe this was the major source of his resilience in a hostile culture. "I, Daniel, perceived in the books the number of years that, according to the word of the LORD to Jeremiah the prophet, must pass before the end of the desolations of Jerusalem, namely, seventy years." (Daniel 9:2) He knew the truth of God's revelation and held fast to that truth, even in very challenging conditions.

When Nebuchadnezzar was ready to kill the wise men of Babylon because they could not interpret his dream, Daniel went to Arioch, the commander of the king's guard, and interceded for these 'wise' men, who were furious and set out to kill Daniel. Now, these men meant nothing to him personally, but he had a compassionate heart and he knew it was wrong to execute them. So, he went to his trusted fellow-Israelites, Hananiah, Mishael and Azariah, and urged them to pray for these men. God then revealed the meaning of the dream to Daniel and the next day he asked Arioch not to kill the wise men, but instead to take him to Nebuchadnezzar because he could interpret the dream.

Talk about sticking your neck out! Daniel was a man of great courage as well as great compassion. He cared about these men, even though they were not fellow-Israelites and indeed were astrologers, sorcerers, and enchanters—men who were doing things directly opposed to God's principles.

It's not easy to have compassion for people sometimes, is it? Especially those who are antagonistic toward us, who have no clue about true spirituality, or whose lifestyles are sinful and against all you know to be right. But as God placed Daniel in the midst of these kinds of people, so he does us today as well, and he does it so we can show God's love and compassion to people who have no clue what it's all about.

Joseph

Joseph was hated by his brothers, flung into a pit to be left for dead, before one enterprising brother saw a business opportunity and sold him to some slave traders who then re-sold him as a household slave to a powerful Egyptian, Potiphar.

Joseph knew he had not been forsaken by God. He worked diligently to serve Potiphar. Joseph was rewarded, and made overseer of his house. Potiphar put the management of his affairs into Joseph's capable hands.

One day when Potiphar was away, Potiphar's wife tried to get Joseph to be her lover. When he refused, she lied and told her husband that Joseph tried to attack her. Joseph was thrown into prison.

Joseph was a good prisoner and the keeper of the prison put him in charge of all the prisoners. He was again betrayed by a butler and had to serve more time.

Throughout all his trials, Joseph remained faithful to God even though he experienced many difficult and unfair circumstances. God's hand was in all of Joseph's circumstances, and the Lord has a clear reason for allowing Joseph to suffer. "As for you, you meant evil against me, but

God meant it for good, to bring it about that many people should be kept alive, as they are today." (Genesis 50:22)

He finally experienced the victory that led to the deliverance of his own people. Joseph sufferings were used by God to deliver many people. Could God also use your sufferings as a witness to people around you?

People around you in the workplace will be watching how you react to tough times. It is exactly when times get tough that the tough can give a good account of the reason for their hope that God has a purpose behind suffering.

C.S. Lewis says, that "Pain insists upon being attended to. God whispers to us in our pleasures, speaks in our consciences, but shouts in our pains. It is his megaphone to rouse a deaf world." [70] Suffering and pain can be an open door for us to enter with the good news which Jesus brings.

Sheep among wolves

When sending out the disciples, Jesus told them; "I am sending you out like sheep among wolves. Therefore, be as shrewd as snakes and as innocent as doves. Be on your guard; you will be handed over to the local councils and be flogged in the synagogues. On my account you will be brought before governors and kings as witnesses to them and to the Gentiles" (Matthew 10:18) This kind of innocent shrewdness is necessary as we are sent out into the common kingdom, often into a hostile environment.

Being in the marketplace as a Christian can be very confusing as the workforce is a combination of sheep and wolves; some of the sheep wear wolves clothing and some of the wolves wear sheep's clothing!

It is not unknown for wolves to form a pack, gang up and set out to make life difficult for you. It is said that one in three people are the target of bullying at work, and even 'mobbing' by a pack.

We need to be shrewd, to be wise in taking our opportunities to speak about Jesus at work. Wisdom is knowing how, and knowing when. "Walk in wisdom toward outsiders, making the best use of the time. Let your speech always be gracious, seasoned with salt, so that you may know how you ought to answer each person.." (Colossians 4:5,6)

Shrewdness also means to be careful to look after your own interests, being cautious and wise, showing good, rational judgment. Our interest in making disciples is a long-term relationship in which we can demonstrate ho the Lord is at work in our lives.

Chapter 5: Discipling in Small Groups

When we read the gospels and observe Jesus' life and ministry we most often notice what he did for the crowds.

He taught them, fed them, healed them, and even John noted that if every work Jesus did while on this earth was written down, the world could not contain the books that would be written. (John 21:25) There's no question that Jesus had and still has a heart for the world!

Because of that, it comes as a surprise to many that amidst all that Jesus did for the masses He spent approximately 85% of His time with just 12 men.

It wasn't because of a lack of care for the masses that Jesus focused on the few…but rather quite the opposite! Jesus focused on the few for the sake of the many! His method for reaching the world was through building deeply into a select few and teaching them to do the same.

Jesus loved everyone, helped many, but invested in just a few. If we hope to take the gospel to the ends of the earth His method must also become our method.

Discipling in small groups

In Matthew 28:16-20, Jesus is talking to a group of disciples. These are the same disciples (apart from Judas) who Jesus moulded and shaped for a three-year period. He had taught them important life lessons as they lived together. Their character development came as they handled conflicts and overcame difficulties together. Jesus had called these disciples to join a new community and become part of a new spiritual family. They learned how to relate to one another through the crucible of conflict. Jesus checked their pride, encouraging them to walk in humility. After three years, they were ready to start the process once again by forming new groups of disciples. They understood that following Jesus meant public confession and a group commitment.

A great way to make disciples is to form a small workplace group. In such a group people from the same organisation can meet together regularly, pray for one another, pray for the organisation they are serving, study the Bible together and relate their findings to their challenges in their work.

A good friend of mine, Martin, organised a workplace group in the headquarters of the Dutch railways. Since it's inception some years ago, this has become a movement to over 200 small groups in businesses, government institutions and other organisations in The Netherlands. A similar movement in the UK, called 'Transform Work,' publishes a list of over 400 workplace groups. [71]

Gathering the group

Jesus gathered a very mixed group of workers into His core group.

There were four in a fishing business; Andrew, John, Simon (Peter) and James. Then there was Levi who was a tax collector; maybe not so popular with the others! Simon the Zealot was a political agitator, who would have certainly wondered at the inclusion of Levi, a Roman collaborator with some rich friends. There was Bartholomew, also known as Nathaniel. His name means 'ploughman', so he was connected in some way with farming. Judas was obviously interested in money, since he was chosen to look after the finances of the group. The Bible provides no information on the professions of Philip, Bartholomew, Thomas, Thaddeus or James.
What a motley collection! Yet with the exception of Judas, Jesus took these men and welded them into a coherent group of Christian believers who were to change the course of the world.

Jesus didn't immediately choose the twelve. He first went to pray about it and this was no short two minute prayer because "he went out to the mountain to pray, and all night he continued in prayer to God." (Luke 6:12) This was an incredibly important decision so Jesus prayed all night long and only then did He receive from the Father confirmation.

The early disciples gathered around Jesus simply because of their trust and love in Him as a person. They were initially attracted by Jesus's personality and what He had to say about the Kingdom of God.

Perhaps that is all that's needed – as one Christian workplace group's key aim read, 'To welcome all those interested in finding out more about the Lord Jesus.' It's as simple as that, but it remains a real challenge for leaders of groups to ensure that the group is seen as united, bringing together people of all personalities and backgrounds, working together, bound by the love of Jesus.

Christian workplace groups continue in the pattern set by that early group of disciples. Any successful group will need development and encouragement and that requires good leadership, but the ultimate effectiveness of the group will not hinge around one person. Leadership within the group can be stressful and tiring and will almost always need to involve more than one person, so when you are setting up a group or trying to develop its activities, don't try to do it all on your own, give some thought to establishing a leadership team. Remember how Jesus developed Peter as a leader for the future.

Praying Together in Groups

One of the key features of workplace groups is the capacity of the group to look outwards beyond its members to the wider needs of the whole organisation and all who work within it. Christian workplace groups do not exist for themselves but for the benefits they can bring into the workplace so that all may share in the joy that Jesus brings

Prayer needs to be the bedrock underpinning all the group does. When praying in the group, it is especially important that the different Christian traditions represented by group members are respected and reflected in how you pray. Some may be prefer silent prayer, others praying out loud either one at a time, or praying out loud together. Vary the type of prayer used, and ensure through discussion and feedback, that all are comfortable. Larger groups can be split into smaller ones to pray.

Topics for prayer might include: the leadership of the workplace, co-workers, the success and growth of the organisation, issues facing the organisation, needs of colleagues – both Christians and non-Christians, growth in the group, needs of members of the group, asking God to reveal what He is calling the group to do…

Use a prayer card in which you write the names of people who the Lord is putting on your heart to pray for.

In our space services company, we made a long list of our employees, customers, suppliers and advisors and prayed for them weekly.

We prayed specifically that the Lord would open a door to speak about Jesus. I was asked to give an interview to a Dutch newspaper about our faith, and how it related to working at a scientific institute like the European Space Agency. I mentioned things like the Bible being our major source of inspiration and guidance for our work, and that we prayed for our employees and customers. The next day, the article was published with the headline, "Praying in a Space Lab."

The European Space Agency has a news-clipping service. The article was captured and sent to all department managers at the Agency! In one go, all our customers go to know about our Christian beliefs. I was actually summoned to the office of the chief contracts officer, who demanded to know why we were bringing religion into a public institution. She was French, and said, "If we were in France, we would take you to court for this." Quite a scary reaction, as we were in the middle of a major contracting proposal round. I explained why our faith in Jesus is so important to us and reminded her that we actually prayed in our office and not at the Agency, with the exception of private prayers walking around the site. There was some consternation around our customers, but the Lord protected our business.

The outcome was that the door was opened so we could share our faith with many customers and employees.

Group Purpose

It is important to set a vision for your group. What are your aims and objectives? Setting a clear direction for the group is not only vitally important for your members, but also for your employers who will want to know what the purpose of your group is.

It is not only important that superiors understand the purpose of your group, but also that the group members themselves understand why they exist. Your group will never be effective in transforming the workplace if the group members do not have a shared understanding of its purpose.

Jesus was absolutely clear about His mission on earth and throughout His ministry took key opportunities to set out His vision, aims and objectives. A key vision statement which Jesus made can be found in Mark 10:45, where He stated; "For even the Son of Man came not to be served but to serve, and to give his life as a ransom for many."

This is a good purpose statement for your workplace group. First of all, seek to serve the interests of your co-workers, and the organisation as whole. Then, to seek ways in which people can be brought to salvation. This can cost a part of your life!

Workplace Alpha

We are not paid to evangelise, but to serve the interests of the organisation we work for. Knowing your employer's workplace policies is a big part of having a positive Christian testimony on your job. If your 'Christian activities,' such as reading your Bible on the job or witnessing, detract from your work, that will not honor Christ or contribute to a positive witness.

Generally, lunchtime is a 'free zone,' and after-work get-togethers or pre-work breakfast meetings are always appropriate, if your co-workers are interested in meeting with you.

The Alpha course provides a practical introduction to the Christian faith and is running in very diverse working environments, ranging from factories to multinational corporations. [72]
It is an opportunity for people of all backgrounds to explore the meaning of life in a familiar and convenient location and is designed to fit into a regular working day, e.g. over a lunch hour or run after work. There are courses running from boardrooms to factories and from local coffee shops to those run through virtual online networks. All the materials for running a course are online, downloadable and easy to use.

My friend, Martin, working at the HQ of the Dutch railways, organised Alpha courses in his own lunchtime so that he did not need his employer's permission. Posters were placed in prominent places (in this case, the refreshment points) with the name of the contact printed on them, and the details were publicised on a website that they created specifically for the event. The most important thing that they did was pray, every week, for people to come along to hear God's message. And they did … many came to faith through Alpha courses at work.

One on one.

I found that breakfast was a wonderful time to meet with a person, study the Bible together and pray. I did this in my office, taking sandwiches from home, in a café over coffee and croissants, or even in someone's home.
I almost always used Biblical principles on specific topics

to discuss with the people I was discipling. These were practical issues like handling money, business dilemma's and work related topics which were normally never discussed in church meetings.

Reading a specific book together can be a great way to disciple someone.

However, I must prefer discipling people in small groups, because of the community and sharing benefits. In fact, most of my one-on-one discipling kind of morphed into small groups, after friends wanting to bring other friends!

Start with one and you will discover more will come!

"Ask God to give you one." [73] The same challenge that Dawson Trotman gave to Les Spencer in 1933 that started The Navigators can be your starting point today.

Some Questions To Consider

The Lord wants us to multiply what we have learned by passing what we have learned on to others, helping them to experience God@Work!
As an old, and very experienced disciple, Paul wrote in his final letter to Timothy; "You then, my child, be strengthened by the grace that is in Christ Jesus, and what you have heard from me in the presence of many witnesses entrust to faithful men, who will be able to teach others also." 2 Timothy 2:1-2)

1. Chapter 1 discusses the commission gave by Jesus to 'go, make disciples.'

> How are you carrying out this commission Jesus gave to you?

2. Look on page 193 at how Jesus used everyday situations to teach people about following Him using financial examples.

> How could you use financial principles or problems to teach others about God's way of managing finances?

3. It is said that people must accept the messenger, before they can accept the message.

> Do you agree with this?

> Why is this so important?

4. Where the darkness is greater, the light shines brighter. Chapter 4 discusses being good news in a challenging environment.

How do you cope with spiritual warfare around financial affairs in your organisation?

5. Jesus disciples his followers mainly in a small group of twelve.

Are you meeting regularly with other believers at work?

Could you start a small group to share problems, pray for people at work, and for opportunities to share Christ, both practically and verbally?

References

1.https://www.barrypopik.com/index.php/new_york_city/
entry/
show_me_your_checkbook_and_ill_tell_you_your_values

2. https://bibleportal.com/bible-quote/finances-the-
heart-give-me-five-minutes-with-a-person-s-checkbook-
and-i-will-tell-you-where-their-heart-is

3. https://bible.org/seriespage/lesson-21-prescription-
contentment-1-timothy-66-8

4 https://www.biblestudytools.com/lexicons/greek/nas/
oikonomos.html

5 https://www.transparency.org/en/gcb

6 https://www.crowe.com/uk/insights/financial-cost-
fraud-data-2021

7 https://www.pwc.com/gx/en/services/forensics/
economic-crime-survey.html

8 https://www.thehrdirector.com/features/miscellaneous/
financial-problems-work-epidemic/

9 https://www.researchgate.net/publication/
335107460_Measuring_Well-
being_and_Sustainability_in_the_Netherlands_the_first_Mo
nitor_of_Well-being

10 https://www.benefitspro.com/2019/10/21/employee-
financial-stress-how-to-recognize-and-address-this-
growing-workplace-problem/?slreturn=20220230095502

11 https://www.spiceworks.com/hr/benefits-
compensation/guest-article/businesses-losing-500-
billion-due-to-employees-financial-stress-2/

12 www.fidelity.com

13 https://www.scribd.com/document/438717703/pwc-2019-employee-wellness-survey-pdf

14. Strong's Concordance of the Bible. Word 1285

15. Strong's concordance, Word 2428

16. Creation, Fall, Redemption and Your Money, an 2010 article by Dr. Tim Keller. Redeemer City to City, used with permission.

17 Theology of Work Project Online Materials by Theology of Work Project, Inc. is licensed under a Creative Commons Attribution-NonCommercial 4.0 International License. Based on a work at www.theologyofwork.org

18 See Deuteronomy 19:14, 27:17; Proverbs 22:28, 23:10; Job 24:2

19 See Mark. 10:9; Luke 18:20, 19:8; Romans 13:9; 1 Corinthians 6:9-10

20. Quoted by Dr. Gary Hoag at https://generositymonk.com/2011/10/22/a-w-tozer-the-monstrous-substitution-in-our-pursuit-of-god/

21 https://www.goodreads.com/author/show/4862.Randy_Alcorn/blog?page=76

22 https://www.epm.org/blog/2018/Jan/17/pastors-model-teach-stewardship

23 . https://archive.org/stream/TheNewBeing/TillichPaul-TheNewBeingexistentialSermonschristianLibrary_djvu.txt Chapter 7

24. Money and Power, Jacques Ellul, 1979. Marshall Pickering. Page 53.

25 https://bibleportal.com/bible-quote/to-clasp-the-hands-in-prayer-is-the-beginning-of-an-uprising-against-the-disorder-of-the-world

26. Money and Power, Jacques Ellul, Marshall Pickering. Page 79.

27. 7 Habits of Highly Successful People, by Stephen R. Covey.

28 https://twitter.com/timkellernyc/status/1040604582248960000?lang=en

29. Les Miserables by Victor Hugo. 1982 Penguin Classics

30. www.youtube.com/watch?v=vzkYfgme2Ps

31. en.wikipedia.org/wiki/Darlington_Bus_War

32. A Christian Theology of Business Ownership, by Bill English. 2021. Chapter 8.

33. Business to the Glory of God, The Bible's Teaching on the Moral Goodness of Business, by Wayne Grudem. Crossway Books. 2003.

34. Every Good Endeavour, Timothy Keller, 2012. Dutton - Penguin Group.

35. Your Work Matters to God, by Douglas Sherman and Howard Hendricks. 1990. Navpress.

36 https://www.goodreads.com/quotes/656313-if-a-man-is-called-to-be-a-street-sweeper

37. Good to Great by Jim Collins. 2001, Harper Collins Publishers

38 https://www.nytimes.com/1970/09/13/archives/a-friedman-doctrine-the-social-responsibility-of-business-is-to.html

39 https://www.economicsummit.eu/wp-content/uploads/2018/04/EoM-CSR-and-CP-nieuw.pdf

40 https://eom.org

41 https://alliesagainstslavery.org/blog-2016-1-18-a-single-garment-of-destiny/

42 https://tifwe.org/what-is-the-purpose-of-your-business/

43 https://hbr.org/2002/02/theyre-not-employees-theyre-people

44. Peter Drucker, The Practice of Management. 2006. Harper Business Books

45 https://thesplendorofthechurch.com/2022/06/20/fr-luca-pacioli-1147-june-1517-the-father-of-accounting-bookkeeping/

46 https://www.forbes.com/sites/jerrybowyer/2017/08/18/the-theology-of-financial-accounting/?sh=73023dafd747

47 https://www.researchgate.net/publication/336777928_Imago_Dei_How_Accountants_Glorify_God

48. https://www.desiringgod.org/articles/render-to-caesar-the-things-that-are-caesars

49 http://docplayer.net/14753526-The-generous-business.html

50. Business God's Way by Howard Dayton. Published by Compass- finances God's way.

51 http://www.amazon.com/Bribery-Corruption-Hwa-Yung/dp/9810845456

52 https://www.cipp.org.uk/resources/news/paygiv.html

53 https://pennies.org.uk/business-force-for-good-partner-success-story-the-entertainer/

54 Alcorn, Randy. Some content taken from Money, Possessions and Eternity: A Comprehensive Guide to What the Bible Says about Financial Stewardship, Generosity, Materialism, Retirement, Financial Planning, Gambling, Debt, and More. Carol Stream, IL: Copyright ©1989, 2003. Used by permission of Tyndale House Publishers. All rights reserved.

55 The 7 Habits of Highly Effective People by Stephen Covey. Page 276. Published by Franklin Covey.

56 The Oxford Pocket Dictionary of Current English

57 https://www.betterup.com/blog/the-secret-behind-how-to-influence-people

58 https://crossworld.ca/blog/details/is-making-disciples-at-work-practical

59 https://crossworld.ca/blog/details/is-making-disciples-at-work-practical

60 https://www.christianity.com/wiki/god/god-in-three-persons-a-doctrine-we-barely-understand-11634405.html

61 To Live and Work, by Christian Schumacher. 1987.Published by Marc Europe

62 https://www.forbes.com/sites/bryanstolle/2014/07/22/vision-without-execution-is-just-hallucination/?sh=57c42e137446

63 "Everything You Have Heard is Wrong!" by Tony Campolo. 1992. Thomas Nelson Publishers.

64 Love is the Killer App: How to Win Business and Influence Friends by Tim Sanders. 2003. Published by Currency.

65 Fruitfulness on the Frontline by Mark Greene. 2014. Published by the London Institute of Contemporary Christianity.

66 https://fs.blog/ethos-logos-pathos/

67 https://www.franklincovey-benelux.com/en/tips-tools/habit-5-seek-first-to-understand-then-to-be-understood/

68 https://brenebrown.com/videos/ted-talk-the-power-of-vulnerability/

69 https://christianworkingwoman.org/wp-content/uploads/2016/12/How-to-Keep-Your-Job-Kit-update.pdf

70 https://www.cslewisinstitute.org/resources/c-s-lewis-on-the-problem-of-pain/

71 https://www.transformworkuk.org/Groups/332366/Transform_Work_UK/Equip/Why_Workplace_Groups/Why_Workplace_Groups.aspx

72 http://alpha.org/

73 https://www.navigators.org/blog/invest-in-a-few/

www.ingramcontent.com/pod-product-compliance
Lightning Source LLC
LaVergne TN
LVHW010319200726
843507LV00010B/1288